JAMES

JAMES

by
VERNON D. DOERKSEN

MOODY PRESS
CHICAGO

The use of selected references from various versions of the Bible in this publication does not necessarily imply publisher endorsement of the versions in their entirety.

Library of Congress Cataloging in Publication Data

Doerksen, Vernon D.
James

Bibliography: p. 141
1. Bible. N.T. James—Commentaries. I. Title.
BS2785.3.D63 1983 227'.9107 83-13395
ISBN 0-8024-0242-9

3 4 5 6 7 Printing/EP/Year 91 90 89 88 87

Printed in the United States of America

CONTENTS

CHAPTER	PAGE
Introduction	7
1. Growing Through Testings *1:1-12*	12
2. Admitting the True Source of Temptations *1:13-18*	28
3. Using the Word for Spiritual Maturing *1:19-27*	39
4. Accepting Others Without Partiality *2:1-13*	51
5. Exhibiting a Productive Faith *2:14-26*	63
6. Controlling the Tongue *3:1-12*	74
7. Demonstrating Godly Wisdom *3:13-18*	85
8. Giving God First Priority *4:1-10*	93
9. Avoiding Presumptuous Behavior *4:11-17*	106
10. Enduring Wrongful Oppression *5:1-11*	114
11. Concluding Counsel *5:12-20*	126
Bibliography	141

INTRODUCTION

"Faith working through love" (Gal. 5:6) could easily be considered the theme of the epistle of James. The author is concerned that his readers understand well the responsibilities of New Testament Christianity. True saving faith must be a vibrant, working faith. James emphasizes that love for God and faith in Him cannot be separated from an active love for one's neighbor. God's will is that the Christian love both God and the children of God. The fruit of genuine faith is unhypocritical love; the product of love is practical works of righteousness and piety. James does not countenance a dead orthodoxy. He agrees with John that the authentic believer is one who does "not love with word or with tongue, but in deed and truth" (1 John 3:18). That is the heart of his epistle.

Though the primary purpose of this commentary is not the so-called introductory matters such as authorship, destination, date, and purpose, those do need to be touched upon briefly.

Authorship

The author is identified as "James, a bond-servant of God and of the Lord Jesus Christ" (1:1). The New Testament mentions five men by the name of James. The most prominent James in the gospels is James the son of Zebedee and brother of John. In the listings of the apostles, he is always included in the first group of four (Matt. 10:2; Mark 3:17; Luke 6:14; Acts 1:13). It is highly unlikely that he was the author, for he suffered martyrdom at the hands of Herod Agrippa I early in the history of the church (A.D. 44; Acts 12:2). He died before he could have achieved a position of leadership such as that enjoyed by the author of James. Further, if he was James the son of Zebedee, he would likely have designated himself as an apostle and not simply "James."

There are three lesser men named James in the New Testament, all of whom have been generally rejected as being the author. James the son of Alphaeus is one of the lesser known disciples. In the four lists of apostles, his name always heads the third group of four (Matt. 10:3; Mark 3:18; Luke 6:15; Acts 1:13). He is never mentioned elsewhere in the New Testament, and there is no evidence that the early church ever assigned the book of James to him. Another James is James the Less, meaning either "the younger" or "the shorter" (Mark 15:40). His mother, Mary, was present at the crucifixion (Matt. 27:56). Some equate him with James the son of Alphaeus though that cannot be proved. An even lesser known man is James the father of the apostle Judas (not Iscariot; Luke 6:16; Acts 1:13). All that is known of him is that one fact.

A fifth James, and by far the most likely author of the epistle, is James the half-brother of Jesus. He was the second oldest of Mary's five sons: Jesus, James, Joseph, Simon, and Judas (Matt. 13:55; Mark 6:3). Early in the ministry of Christ, Jesus' brothers did not comprehend His messianic ministry (Mark 3:21, 31; John 7:3-6), but evidently after the resurrection James and his brothers became believers (Acts 1:14; 1 Cor. 15:7). He rose to prominence to become the acknowledged leader of the mother church in Jerusalem early in its history (Acts 12:17; 15:12-29; 21:18-25; Gal. 1:18-19; 2:6-9). He appears to have been the moderator of the Jerusalem Council (Acts 15:12-29). The author of the epistle of Jude identifies himself as the "brother of James" (Jude 1).

Several things argue for the traditional position that James the brother of our Lord was the author of the epistle that bears his name. There is a marked similarity in language between the epistle and the speech and letter of Acts 15. The epistle is flavored with Old Testament imagery, which is consistent with James as a leader in a largely Jewish church. In his *Antiquities of the Jews* Josephus makes mention of James as the brother of Jesus and says that his martyrdom by stoning was condemned by the more equitable of the Jews.[1] James's heavy emphasis on righteous living fits well with the tradition that he was called "the Just," and that his knees were like the knees of camels because he spent so much time kneeling in prayer.[2] The admittedly Hebrew tone of the epistle argues for an author steeped in Jewish history and appreciation for the Old Testament. The epistle bears a close similarity to much of Christ's teaching, especially the Sermon on the Mount. The traditional position that the author is James the brother of Jude and half-brother of Jesus commends itself as the correct one.

Destination

The readers are designated as "the twelve tribes who are dispersed abroad" (1:1). The "twelve tribes" is a designation indicating the entirety of the Jewish nation. There are several indications that James is writing to ethnic Jews. Their group is called an "assembly" (lit., "synagogue," 2:2); they unflinchingly adhere to monotheism (2:19); they have an appreciation for the law, the royal law (2:8); and references to Abraham, Rahab, and Elijah suggest Jewish readership. These Jews were those who were "dispersed abroad." The *Dispersion* (scattering) was a term used of Jews living outside of Palestine (see 1 Pet. 1:1). When Jesus reported that He would be leaving, the Jews wondered if He was "intending to go to the Dispersion among the Greeks" (John 7:35). Evidently James, the acknowledged leader of the Jerusalem church, was writing to Jewish believers outside of Jerusalem. They were probably a group living not far from Judea, perhaps in Syria. The readers would be familiar with James and

---

1. Flavius Josephus, "The Antiquities of the Jews," in *The Works of Flavius Josephus,* trans. William Whiston (Edinburgh: William P. Nimmo, n.d.), 423 [Book 20, Chapter 9, Paragraph 1].
2. Eusebius Pamphilus, *The Ecclesiastical History of Eusebius Pamphilus,* trans. Christian Frederick Cruse (Grand Rapids: Baker, 1962), 75-79 [Book 2, Chapter 23].

with some of the illustrations he used such as "scorching wind" (1:11); "fresh and bitter water" (3:11); figs, olives, and vines (3:12); and "early and late rains" (5:7).

Date

James was probably the earliest New Testament epistle written. The Jewish congregation was still meeting in a synagogue (2:2), and the controversy concerning Judaizers and legalism had evidently not yet surfaced. James uses the law in a moral sense, not in the legalistic sense. It appears that the believers were old enough in the Lord that their zeal for Him had begun to wane. Persecution had not yet broken out in a full-scale manner. The organization of the body seems to have been loose (3:1), though there were elders (5:14). The structure of the church was probably patterned after the Jewish synagogue. Because there is no counsel about social relationships between Jews and Gentiles, a subject found in many other New Testament epistles, it would seem that the epistle must have been written sometime before the Jerusalem Council, when issues related to the works of the law came to a head. James portrays Christianity as the consummation of Judaism, the fulfillment of the Old Testament, the law of love from the heart. His ethical emphasis on neighborly concern continues to be a timely message for all ages.

Purpose

James is a pastoral letter written by one deeply concerned with the spiritual well-being of the flock. It is a letter both of encouragement and rebuke: a practical challenge to encourage the godly to live up to their faith and a rebuke to the backsliders to return to a productive faith. It appears that James had received word concerning the flock and wrote this letter in response to particular issues: trials, the use of the tongue, merciful conduct, the uncertainty of life, the problem of poverty, and the need for patient endurance.

The letter was written during the infancy of the church. It is a challenge to live the Christian life, not just profess to it. James assumes his readers are Christians—they have responded by faith to the Lord of Glory. In light of their professed faith, he urges them to live out that faith in deeds of piety. A proper understanding of Paul's "faith without works" and James's "faith with works" is a protection against most doctrinal and practical error. James wants authentic Christian action—his plea is for productive Christianity.

1

GROWING THROUGH TESTINGS

JAMES 1:1-12

James begins his letter with the customary New Testament practice of a three-part salutation: the author, the recipient, and the greeting. Any or all three of those parts could be expanded to suit the particular needs of the author. James amplifies the first two members, but the third part contains the single word "greetings."

James could have identified himself as the Lord's brother (Matt. 13:55; Mark 6:3; Gal. 1:19), or by his ecclesiastic position as the leader of the Jerusalem congregation (Acts 12:17; 15:13; 21:18; Gal. 2:12); but he chose rather to portray himself as "James, a bond-servant of God and of the Lord Jesus Christ." His brother Jude also designated himself a "bond-servant" (Jude 1), as did Paul (Titus 1:1), Peter (2 Pet. 1:1), and John (Rev. 1:1). For the Christian to be a bond-servant or slave portrays not the inhumane, forced, involuntary submission so often the case in human slavery, but rather a willing submission and obedience to the service of Jesus Christ the Lord (Rom. 6:16-23). James recognized that he had been purchased and that he was now a bondservant to the one who had purchased him (1 Cor. 6:20; 1 Pet. 1:18-19). To be a slave of God is not degrading; it is a high privilege.

James saw himself as a bondservant "of God and of the Lord Jesus Christ." In characteristic New Testament style, the Father and the Son are named together in the salutation (Phil. 1:2; 1 Thess. 1:1). That is not the proverbial serving of two masters (Matt. 6:24), for the two are one (John 10:30), and to serve the one is to serve the other (John 5:17; 9:4; 17:4). James, an avid monotheist (2:19), here subtly affirms his belief in the Trinity and reminds his Jewish readers that Jesus the Messiah must be served equally with the Lord God.

The full title ("Lord Jesus Christ") conveys many things about Jesus. To the Jewish reader the ascription "Lord" would signify deity, for in the Old Testament *Yahweh* is translated by the term "Lord" (Ex. 6:2-3; Gr. *kurios*). Several Old Testament quotations that contain the name *Jehovah* (or *Yahweh*) are applied directly to Christ in the New Testament (cf. Rom. 10:9, 13 with Joel 2:32; and 1 Pet. 3:14-15 with Isa. 8:12-13). The title *Lord* also denoted sovereignty. Christ is to be both worshiped and served. The name *Jesus* is equivalent to the Old Testament name *Joshua,* meaning "savior." To Joseph the angel said, "You shall call His name Jesus, for it is He who will save His people from their sins" (Matt. 1:21). That is the name given Him at the incarnation, and it speaks of His humanity. *Christ* is the Greek term for the Hebrew word *Messiah* (John 1:41; 4:25). As such, Jesus is the "Anointed One," the one who fulfills the messianic prophecies (Ps. 2:2; Dan. 9:25). He is the long-expected deliverer, the one who is to establish the Davidic kingdom. It is interesting that only here and in 2:1 does James employ the compound title. Elsewhere he simply uses "Lord."

Two things are said about the recipients of this letter: they are of the twelve tribes, and they are in the Dispersion. The twelve tribes represent the whole physical seed of Jacob, both the northern and the southern kingdoms. The northern tribes of Israel were dispersed after the Assyrian conquest in 722 B.C. (2 Kings 18:9-12), and the southern kingdom was carried into Babylonian captivity in stages between 605 and 586 B.C. (2 Kings 24-25). Under Cyrus, king of Persia, many Jews returned and joined with the remnant that remained in the land (2 Chron. 36:22-23). In New Testament times there were two groups of Israelites: Jews living in Palestine and Jews living throughout the Roman Empire, sometimes called Hellenists. The epithet "the Dispersion" refers to those Jews who were scattered like grain throughout the world. In addition to the scattering because of conquests, Jews had migrated to the four corners of the earth for commercial and other reasons. Luke indicates that at Pentecost there were Jewish people of the Dispersion from "every nation under heaven" who had come to Jerusalem for the feast (Acts 2:5).

It is not certain whether James was writing to the entire Dispersion or to a limited segment of it. Because he has certain subjects in mind and is addressing definite issues, it seems that he is writing to a specific group, perhaps certain Christian Jews living outside of Palestine but still within the province of Syria.

This brief salutation closes with the simple "greetings" (lit., "to rejoice, to be glad"). It was used in the letter of the Jerusalem Council, a document probably written primarily by James (Acts 15:23), and in the letter of Claudius Lysias to Felix (Acts 23:26). The greeting "to rejoice" prepares the readers for the discussion of joy and trials that immediately follows.

Following his brief salutation, James plunges immediately into the subject of trials, counseling his readers to count it all joy when encountering them. James follows with four reasons they should rejoice: trials properly faced develop maturity (1:2-4); trials drive us to God (1:5-8); trials force us to make a proper evaluation of life (1:9-11); and the endurance of trials brings the crown of life (1:12).

TRIALS PROPERLY FACED DEVELOP MATURITY (1:2-4)

The readers were facing difficulties of such magnitude that their faith was being tested. James counseled them to "consider it all joy" when confronting trials. In like manner Peter exhorted his readers, who were being "distressed by various trials," to "greatly rejoice" (1 Pet. 1:6). Neither James nor Peter defined the nature of those trials, but it can be assumed that they were both external pressures, such as afflictions and persecutions, and the annoyances and griefs of everyday life.

Contrary to the natural fleshly response to difficulties, these Christians were challenged to consider such experiences as a basis for all joy. That joy is not to be confused with a happiness or pleasure that is dependent on outward circumstances. Rather, Christian joy is, as Adamson says, "a man's pleasure in his *(and his brothers')* progress toward Christian salvation."[1] "Consider" means careful, deliberate judgment. The readers are encouraged to evaluate carefully their trials, knowing that from negative experiences Christian growth can take place. For that reason they can rejoice in the face of hardships.

"All joy," in the emphatic position, forms an interesting bridge to the salutation. Having just written "greetings," or "to rejoice" (*chairein*), James challenged his readers to assess their various trials as a basis for joy (*charan*). "All" joy speaks of pure joy, unmixed joy, joy to the highest. Perhaps James used "all joy" as a balance or counterpart to "various trials." Christian joy can be as intense and pure as trials can be varied.

The term translated "trials" (*peirasmoi*) is a word of considerable breadth. It is used both of adversities that plague man within and without and of inner enticements to sin. Often those two meanings, "trials" and "temptations," are closely related. What God permits as a test to develop character in His child, Satan or the flesh may use as a temptation. No doubt when God tested Abraham by commanding him to offer his son (Gen. 22:1), Satan tempted him not to obey God's command. It is interesting that God used the evil designs of Satan against righteous Job to build Job's character. "Various trials" are permitted by God to develop character, though the flesh may use those same problems as a temptation or enticement to sin (1:13). When trials come the believer will react in one of two ways: he will either grow in Christian character or he will become embittered, rebellious,

---

1. James B. Adamson, *The Epistle of James, The New International Commentary on the New Testament,* ed. F. F. Bruce (Grand Rapids: Eerdmans, 1981), 53.

and hardhearted. James assumes the best of his readers (cf. Heb. 6:9) and exhorts them to rejoice because character development will come.

Fifteen times in this short epistle James addresses his readers as "my brethren" or "brethren." He sees them as fellow members in the spiritual family of faith, not merely fellow Israelites. From the start James seeks to identify with them as a brother in their sufferings. By being genuinely concerned about them in their trials and gaining credibility as a caring family member, he will later be able to rebuke them severely in certain problem areas, such as partiality (2:1-13), lifeless faith (2:14-26), uncontrolled speech (3:1-12), and dissensions in the body (4:1-6).

Those varied trials are not to be understood as troubles of one's own making, but rather those of an unavoidable nature. They are trials into which believers fall. Also, it is not an issue of "*if* they come," but rather "*when* they come." Paul reminds us that those who desire to be godly will suffer persecution (2 Tim. 3:12).

It is easier to understand having joy follow sorrow than having joy during the difficulty. In Scripture we read both of rejoicing after calamity and during calamity. Christ told His disciples that as joy follows the sorrows of childbirth, so also the disciples' sorrow would be turned to joy when they saw Him again (John 16:20-22). Of Jesus it is written, "For the joy set before Him [He] endured the cross" (Heb. 12:2). And the disciples rejoiced "that they had been considered worthy to suffer shame for His name" (Acts 5:41). Here also the reader is commanded to consider trials as a basis for joy.

A reason for the joy is that the trials that test the believer's faith will produce endurance (v. 3), which in turn will develop Christian maturity (v. 4). "Knowing" suggests that the readers were not ignorant of that truth, but in times of difficulty they needed to be reminded again that hardships produce character. The "testing" of faith can be understood in one of two ways. It may mean the approved part of faith, hence the genuine part, that part of faith that has passed the test. The idea would be that that which is genuine in faith will produce patience. On the other hand, it may speak of the means of testing: trials are a means or an instrument whereby faith is tested; they cleanse and purify faith. The context seems to argue for the second position. Faith is tested by trials.

Throughout the epistle, James has much to say about a living, vibrant faith. For one thing, genuine faith does not evaporate in the face of difficulties. Meeting obstacles and overcoming them proves the genuineness of faith and molds character. That developing character or virtue is called "endurance." The testing of faith "produces endurance." The present tense indicates a continuous action. "Endurance," or "patience" as it is sometimes translated, is more than passive endurance and quiet submission. It is rather that active steadfastness and staying power that confronts difficulties and continues on in faith with purpose and resolve. James uses the same term to describe the character of Job (5:11). His "endurance" allowed him to say, "The Lord gave and the Lord has taken away. Blessed be the name of the Lord" (Job 1:21), and, "Shall we indeed accept good from God and not accept adversity?" (Job 2:10). The verb form of the word is also used in 1:12: "Blessed is the man who *perseveres* under trial" (italics added).

But endurance or steadfastness is not the end result; it is rather an important step toward Christian maturity (v. 4). The readers are challenged to allow steadfastness to have its perfect result. That "perfect result" can be understood in one of two ways. It may mean the development of perfect endurance or the development of perfect character. The second meaning is more appropriate; perfect endurance should result in perfect character. "Result" is the noun form of the verb "produce" (v. 3). As testing produces endurance, so endurance should have its product. The adjective "perfect" is used five times by James (twice here; 1:17, 25; 3:2). It speaks of completeness, maturity, full-grown, brought to its end, finished. Impatience, complaining, or bitterness would not be a "perfect" result. The command is in the present tense, indicating continuous and progressive action. The purposes for testing are being accomplished as we remain steadfast.

The outcome of a proper attitude toward trials is threefold, two positives and one negative: "That you may be perfect and complete, lacking in nothing." Paul writes that "tribulation brings about perseverance; and perseverance, proven character; and proven character, hope" (Rom. 5:3-4). "Perfect" and "complete" are in some ways synonymous, but are not without their individual shades of meaning. To be "perfect" means to be mature, fully developed. In this setting it could not mean absolute perfection; rather, it is that goal of full development to which every Christian should aspire. It is adulthood as opposed to childhood. The writer to the Hebrews urges his readers to "press on to maturity [perfection]" (Heb. 6:1).

The second term, "complete," means entire, every part intact. Every part of the Christian character is being developed. In the growth and maturation of the physical body, normal growth means that every individual part of the body is growing to its mature size. So in the development of the spiritual person, every aspect of the spiritual life, in all its parts, must mature. As in the bearing of the fruit of the Spirit, one will not have one virtue without the other eight (Gal. 5:22-23).

Not only will the one who endures testing be perfect and complete, he will also be "lacking in nothing." To lack is the exact opposite of being complete. All areas of the personality need to grow, and these testings will provide a means whereby growth will take place. No area in Christian development will be in want.

The Christian's approach to difficulties is the opposite of the world's. The Christian considers them joy: "For those whom the Lord loves He disciplines, and He scourges every son whom He receives" (Heb. 12:6), and, "Every branch that bears fruit, He prunes it, that it may bear more fruit" (John 15:2). The one who wants to be "perfect and complete, lacking in nothing" must endure, being steadfast, in the face of testing.

TRIALS DRIVE US TO GOD (1:5-8)

As the believer encounters trials, he will not always know how to react to them and will need wisdom from above. Wisdom is important in the maturing process of the individual. It could be an area where there is incompleteness. That lack can be met by believing, unwavering prayer to a God who freely gives.

"Lacks" provides the bridge from the previous verse's "lacking in nothing." The repetition of a word or its cognate to introduce a new thought or a progression of thoughts is characteristic of James's style. The technique is used several times in the immediate context: "greetings" (v. 1, *chairein*) and "joy" (v. 2, *charan*); "endurance" (v. 3) and "endurance" (v. 4); "lacking" (v. 4) and "lacks" (v. 5); "ask" (v. 5) and "ask" (v. 6); and "doubting" (v. 6) and "doubts" (v. 6). That same linguistic style, called *paronomasia,* occurs also in 1:12-15; 21-25; 3:2-8; and 4:1-3.

The lack James addresses here is wisdom. He assumes it as a real need. Verse 5 could be translated, "If any of you lacks wisdom, and he does, let him ask of God." "Wisdom" is a key word with James. It occurs again in 3:13, 15, and 17. To James "wisdom is 'the principal thing,' to which he gives the same prominence as St. Paul to faith, St. John to love, St. Peter to hope."[2] For the Christian, wisdom is more than the ability to follow obtruse arguments, to know a series of facts, or to have mental sagacity. It is rather keen spiritual discernment, which enables the believer to make correct moral judgments and face life with its trials in a way consistent with the revealed will of God. Solomon wrote, "The fear of the Lord is the beginning of wisdom" (Prov. 9:10). For the Christian, wisdom starts with an acknowledgment of God and a readiness to perform His will. Such wisdom will be in conflict with the wisdom of this world, for the world's wisdom is "earthly, natural, demonic" (3:15).

---

2. Joseph B. Mayor, *The Epistle of St. James, Classic Commentary Library* (Grand Rapids: Zondervan, 1954), 38.

The wisdom from above is God's gift to man, not an accomplishment of human ingenuity or skill. The child of God who senses a lack of and need for wisdom is commanded to express his need to God. The believer has the Scriptures, but he needs the constant illumination of the Scripture that only God can give. "Ask" is in the present tense, meaning "keep on asking." The same form is used in Matthew 7:7, "Ask [keep on asking], and it shall be given to you." The parable of the importunate widow was given to teach believers "that at all times they ought to pray and not to lose heart" (Luke 18:1).

The one who seeks wisdom asks of "God, who gives." "Gives" is a participle with the definite article, and it may relate to "God" in one of two ways. It may be used in apposition, "God, the one who gives," or it may be "the giving God." The second meaning implies that giving is part of the nature of God. The present tense of the participle suggests that our God is continually giving. As we are to be continually asking, He is continually giving. The Christian can be assured, though, that whatever the need—wisdom or otherwise—our God is a perpetually giving God. "It is this view of the nature of God which encourages the believer to come boldly to God with his requests."[3]

The extent of His giving is "to all," and the manner is "generously and without reproach." God's common grace, like rain and fruitful seasons (Acts 14:17), is for all mankind, but James is addressing not all mankind, but Christians. It is to Christians who ask that God grants the request. The "all" is limited to all who ask. The manner in which it is granted is expressed in a positive and a negative form, "generously and without reproach." "Generously" has been variously interpreted. It may mean to give simply; to give with a single motive. In that sense God gives out of the single and pure motive of aiding the asker. He does not have secondary or ulterior motives. Or it may mean that God gives without

---

3. D. Edmond Hiebert, *The Epistle of James* (Chicago: Moody, 1979), 81.

restraint; He gives abundantly and liberally. Both concepts are true. God gives to all generously and He gives wholeheartedly.

Further, God not only gives abundantly, He also gives "without reproach." Gifts can lose their joy if with them come rebuke, embarrassment, and humiliation. The believer is not continually scolded for misusing a previous gift, nor is the gift given in such a grudging way that one is embarrassed to accept it. God does not humiliate us for our continual lack of adequately or properly using the wisdom He provides. When we ask, He stands ready to help us again and again. There is no end to His mercy. That does not provide an excuse for negligence or failure to appropriate His grace, but it should encourage us constantly to seek the Lord for wisdom and His other gifts.

The request, though, must be made in faith (v. 6). Faith, for James, is not just a belief in the existence of God. That even the demons confess (2:19). Nor is it merely a body of doctrine. It is a deep conviction that God "is, and that He is a rewarder of those who seek Him" (Heb. 11:6), coupled with an acknowledgment of our need for help. We must believe not only in God's ability to respond to our petition, but also His willingness to do so in conformity to His nature and will. The present imperative "ask" suggests perseverance in prayer. This exhortation on prayer is reminiscent of the teachings of Christ: we are to ask (Matt. 7:7), in faith (Mark 11:24), with perseverance (Luke 18:1-8).

The antithesis to faith is doubt; we are to ask "without any doubting." "Doubting" speaks not of uncertainty but of internal indecision. It is wavering between two competing desires: self-interests and God's interests. That doubting suggests a reluctance to commit oneself wholly to God's care. The same expression was used by the Spirit when He commanded Peter to go visit Cornelius, "Arise, go downstairs, and accompany them without misgivings" (Acts 10:20). One may doubt because he is not fully assured that God will respond, or because he is not sure he wants God to answer.

The doubting petitioner is pictured as the unsettled, unstable waves of the sea. The simile is that of a violent, wind-driven, turbulent storm out in the ocean. That is in vivid contrast to the individual resting securely by faith in the Lord. The two participles, "driven" and "tossed," are in the present tense, suggesting continuous agitation. The passive voice suggests an outside force. Doubters lack the inner stability to withstand external forces; therefore they are in constant turmoil and indecision.

Not only does the doubter lack stability, he also disqualifies himself from being a recipient of God's special favor (v. 7). He should not imagine that anything different should be the case. By the use of the demonstrative pronoun, "*that* man," James places himself at a distance from such a one. It has a somewhat disdainful savor. The Greek negative implies that that man should stop "entertaining any thought of receiving an answer to his prayer."[4] "The Lord" could have reference to Christ or to God the Father. "Lord" is a title for Christ in verse 1, but here the nearer context of "God" (v. 5) would argue that "Lord" refers to God the Father.

Translations of verse 8 vary. In the original there is no verb expressed, so some translations add the verb "is," whereas others make the whole verse appositional to "that man." If the verb is supplied, it may read, "He *is* a double-minded man, unstable in all he does" (NIV), or, "A double-minded man *is* unstable in all his ways" (KJV). If it is used appositionally, it would simply follow verse 7, "a double-minded man, unstable in all his ways" (ASV), or, "*being* a double-minded man, unstable in all his ways" (NASB). The ASV retains the terseness characteristic of James and perhaps reflects most accurately the meaning. It is a further description of that man who lacks faith and conviction in prayer.

"Double-minded" is literally "two-souled," almost as if the man has two personalities in constant conflict with each other. That term is used only here and in 4:8 in the New

4. Ibid., 86.

Testament; perhaps it is a word coined by James. He may have had Psalm 12:2, "with double heart they speak," in mind. For the Christian, divided loyalty is inappropriate; there must be a singleness of mind. Jesus warned, "No one can serve two masters. . . . You cannot serve God and mammon" (Matt. 6:24). In the New Testament the word translated "unstable" occurs only here and in 3:8 ("restless"). Double-mindedness will express itself in unstableness in every area of life, not only in prayer. True Christianity affects every part of our existence. Singlemindedness gives one confidence in prayer and direction in life.

TRIALS FORCE US TO MAKE A PROPER EVALUATION OF LIFE (1:9-11)

The connection between this paragraph and the preceding is along two lines. There is an easy tie between "glory" (v. 9) and "joy" (v. 2). Just as the Christian is to rejoice in face of trials, knowing the personal benefits that will come, so also he has grounds to glory. There is also a close relationship between the "double-minded man" (v. 8) and the "rich man" (v. 10). As the double-minded man has divided loyalties, so the rich man is torn between his submission to God and his love for earthly possessions. Double-mindedness and instability prevent joyous confidence in God, and keeping an eye on worldly benefits tends to cloud the greatness and glory of our spiritual condition in Christ.

Both rich and poor are found in the church, but neither wealth nor poverty is a determining factor in spirituality. The church is a fellowship of believers from all walks of life and levels of society. We are all equal in Christ. The believer's attitude toward wealth will say much about his spirituality.

The man of humble circumstances is called a "brother" (v. 9). That subtlety reminds us that the church is a family. In a family there is a basic equality among the members, even though there may be differences in such areas as aptitude, abilities, and resources. The early church was filled with poor people (Acts 2:45; 4:35; 1 Cor. 1:26-28) and slaves (Eph. 6:5; Col. 3:22), who in the eyes of the world were nobodies. But they should not resent their position, for in Christ they have been exalted to a "high position." That does not mean the brother has become physically rich, but rather that he is spiritually well off. He is a prince.

The word translated "glory" is usually translated as "boast." It can be used in both a good and a bad sense. It can convey the idea of self-congratulation and arrogance, a bragging about what one is or has achieved. In the good sense, the believer should boast not in himself, but in God (Rom. 5:11; 1 Cor. 1:31), in the cross (Gal. 6:14), in the hope of salvation (Rom. 5:2), and in tribulation and weaknesses because of what God can do through them (Rom. 5:3; 2 Cor. 12:9). A downcast, insecure, threatened Christian is not the norm. A believer can be justly proud and hold his head high because of his position. Though his outward social status may be viewed with contempt by the world, the poverty-stricken believer can rejoice in his spiritual status, which is based in his relationship to Christ.

The sentence continues with a consideration of the rich man (v. 10). Some feel that the rich man is an unbeliever because of what James says in verse 11, and what he says about the rich in 2:5-7 and 5:1-6. But the oppressive rich mentioned in 2:5-7 and 5:1-6 are not necessarily to be equated with the "rich man" here. In these verses James merely contrasts the rich Christian with the poor Christian. The parallel construction of the two verses indicates that both the noun "brother" and the verb "glory" go with both individuals. Wealth has its dangers (Matt. 19:23; Luke 18:22-27), but it can be used properly and beneficially (Acts 4:37; 11:29; 1 Tim. 6:17-19; 1 John 3:17). Rich Christians can be a blessing to the church, but they must have the right inner attitude toward wealth. The humiliation of the rich man is figurative, indicating an attitude of heart. As the poor man is spiritually elevated, so the rich man is spiritually humbled. His former pride in wealth is shattered as he realizes its true worth. Lenski writes, "As the poor brother forgets all his earthly poverty, so the rich brother forgets all his earthly riches."[5]

James follows with the general truth applicable to all who put their trust in riches: the fleeting, transitory nature of human existence. He quotes from Isaiah 40:6-7 to emphasize that physical life is brief in contrast to more lasting spiritual values. Paul fully recognized that reality when he wrote of his experience, "I count all things to be loss in view of the surpassing value of knowing Christ Jesus my Lord, for whom I have suffered the loss of all things, and count them but rubbish in order that I may gain Christ" (Phil. 3:8; cf. Jer. 9:23-24).

The imagery used for the brevity of life is the "flowering grass," a frequent figure in Scripture (Ps. 90:5-6; Isa. 51:12). Four verbs—rises, withers, falls off, is destroyed—describe the rapid demise of the flowering grass when the hot desert wind, the *sirocco,* blows on it (v. 11). The grassy hillside with all the wild flowers can be a sight of immense simple beauty, but the sudden dry desert wind blowing from the Negev will almost instantaneously reduce the vegetation from its former glory to withered grass and blowing petals. In like manner the rich man will fade away.

The verse ends in a similar way to the ending of verse 10. But here the added emphasis is on the rich man "in the midst of his pursuits." "Pursuits" may refer to literal travel, or it may have the metaphorical meaning of "business." The idea seems to be that the rich man will pass away in the midst of his restless business pursuits. Physical death will overtake him as he chases the elusive dollar.

THE ENDURANCE OF TRIALS BRINGS THE CROWN OF LIFE (1:12)

James now draws a fitting conclusion to what he has said about trials. It also serves as an introduction to what follows. Because "trial" (*peirasmon;* cf. v. 2) may mean either trial in

---

5. R. C. H. Lenski, *The Interpretation of the Epistle to the Hebrews and the Epistle of James* (Minneapolis: Augsburg, 1966), 535.

the sense of an adversity or affliction, or temptation in the sense of enticement to sin, the reader is left to decide which of the two James meant. Is it the one who endures temptation that is blessed? Or is it the one who endures adversity? This verse seems to provide a bridge between those two meanings. The trials faced (v. 2) can actually become a temptation (v. 13). The believer can endure trial, come forth victorious, not yielding to the temptations of the flesh that spring forth in time of adversity. God always provides an avenue of escape (1 Cor. 10:13).

"Blessed," meaning "happy," is the same word used in the Sermon on the Mount (Matt. 5:3-11; cf. Luke 6:20-23). It denotes an inner quality of life, a peace, contentment, or satisfaction that can be sustained in spite of adverse external difficulties. It is not so much an emotional feeling of happiness as it is a state of blessedness experienced in this life by citizens of God's kingdom and to be more fully realized in the future life. That blessedness comes not in freedom from trials, but rather through the endurance of testings. "Persevere" carries the idea of endurance, to hold up under pressure, to be steadfast, to stand firm. The noun form of the verb is used in verses 3 and 4. The believer is to consider it joy when he encounters trials because of the resultant endurance produced (v. 3); now he is said to be blessed when he endures. The results of endurance in the earlier verses are spiritual growth and maturity in the present life.

"Approved" was the term used for the testing of coins when determining their genuineness (the noun form is used in v. 3). The aorist participle suggests that the test is over and the person has been demonstrated to be a genuine believer. As the believer steadfastly endures each trial and temptation that comes his way, there is increased proof of his faithfulness to God and the genuineness of his character.

The crown of life is the reward. The Bible often speaks of rewards to be received at the end of this life. Of the persecuted Jesus said, "Your reward in heaven is great" (Matt. 5:12). Paul speaks of one's reward as being in accordance with one's work (1 Cor. 3:14). Often the reward is expressed as a victory's crown or trophy, an award that would come to the winner of an athletic event (1 Cor. 9:25; 2 Tim. 4:8; 1 Pet. 5:4; Rev. 2:10). The trophy mentioned in this context is the crown or trophy of life. "Life" is appositional, in other words, the crown that is life. It also has the article, the crown of *the* life, indicating the eternal life that awaits the believer.

That crown that is eternal life has been promised to those who love Him. The name "Lord" is not in the original, though it is self-evident that James has the Lord in mind as the one who made the promise. There are many biblical promises of life in Scripture, but this specific promise is noted elsewhere in Scripture only in Revelation 2:10. James may have had reference to the general tenor of Scripture, or perhaps he had in mind a saying of Jesus not recorded in the gospel accounts (cf. Acts 20:35). Eternal life is assured, for it is "promised." The God who cannot lie has given His word. He cannot be unfaithful to His promise (2 Tim. 2:13; Titus 1:2; Heb. 6:18). It is "those who love Him" who are the recipients of this promise of life. That is a frequent designation of the people of God; of the Old Testament saints (Ex. 20:6; Deut. 7:9; Ps. 145:20) and the New Testament believers (Rom. 8:28; 1 Cor. 2:9). Implicit in the concept of love is obedience. To love God is to obey Him (1 John 2:5-6; 5:3). The Christian who is undergoing difficult times can rejoice on two counts; in the present life he is being perfected, and for the future he has the promise of life.

2

ADMITTING THE TRUE SOURCE OF TEMPTATIONS

JAMES 1:13-18

A trial can easily become a temptation. God's purpose in trials is our growth into maturity, but we can react with bitterness and hardness of heart. The writer to the Hebrews encouraged his readers to consider the persecutions they were enduring as the Father's loving discipline of His children. The product to be achieved was "the peaceful fruit of righteousness" (Heb. 12:11). There is always the danger of a "root of bitterness springing up" (Heb. 12:15) when adversities are not responded to in the proper manner.

Perhaps some of James's readers had failed in their Christian walk when they had encountered trials; perhaps they had not rejoiced in light of their spiritual standing, but had complained about their earthly circumstances. Perhaps they were putting too much emphasis on their transitory earthly existence and were not concerned enough about eternal values. It is possible that some had succumbed to the lure of the licentious world around them. When we have failed in any of those areas, or in a host of others, our tendency is to blame something or someone outside ourselves. The one who has yielded to sin must face up to his personal responsibility and guilt. James addresses the issue in three parts: God is not to be blamed for temptation (1:13), the source of temptation is lust (1:14-15), and God brings good, not sin (1:16-18).

GOD IS NOT TO BE BLAMED FOR TEMPTATION (1:13)

As noted above, when one yields to temptation the natural inclination is to blame another and often ultimately to blame God. When God confronted Adam with his sin, Adam responded, "The woman whom Thou gavest to be with me, she gave me from the tree, and I ate" (Gen. 3:12). Evidently some of the readers were accusing God of tempting them. They might argue that since God sends trials, He is responsible for the temptations to sin that have been aroused by those trials. James is not denying that God tries men, but he denies that God tries with evil intent. No one should entertain such a thought and thereby excuse himself for his behavior. The present imperative with the negative suggests that those claiming to be tempted by God should immediately stop making such an accusation.

The one who has yielded to temptation blatantly seeks to absolve his guilt by saying, "I am being tempted by God." The preposition "by" (*apo*) may suggest a remote source. In that sense, the person is not necessarily saying that God is the immediate cause or the one who is directly doing the enticing, but rather that God is behind whatever has brought the individual to the situation in which he is being tempted. In like manner Adam blamed Eve directly, and God indirectly, for his own failure. Far be it from God to entice to sin; rather He has promised that when we are tempted He will not allow the temptation to be stronger than we can endure, and along with it He has promised a way of escape (1 Cor. 10:13).

James gives two reasons it is incorrect to blame God for temptations. One is based on His character, and the other on His actions: "God cannot be tempted" and "He Himself does not tempt." The first clause may be taken in either an active or a passive sense. It may mean "God does not tempt," or it may mean "God is not tempted." Because the next clause teaches that God does not tempt, the active sense would be redundant. God is of such a righteous, holy, good, and perfect character that He is not susceptible to temptation.

James avows without argument that there is absolutely nothing in God to which evil can make its appeal. That he is speaking of enticement and solicitation to do evil is clear from the phrase "by evil." Some have suggested that the meaning is "God is untried in evil," in the sense of being inexperienced in evil. Though that is surely true, the context seems to argue for temptation. God is untemptable; He cannot be solicited or enticed to sin.

The second reason God cannot be blamed is that God "does not tempt any one." Because of His character He does not tempt, nor *can* He tempt. His holy character would not allow Him to do what is morally wrong. The statement is intensive; God "Himself" does not tempt. There are certain passages that speak of God's testing. He tested Abraham (Gen. 22:1) and Israel (Ex. 16:4; Judg. 2:22), but that was to build character, not to solicit evil. Even in the so-called Lord's Prayer, the request "Do not lead us into temptation" has sometimes been translated, "Do not bring us to the test" (Matt. 6:13, NEB*).

THE SOURCE OF TEMPTATION IS LUST (1:14-15)

Having forthrightly rejected the notion that God is the source of temptation, James declares that lust is the culprit. "Each one" suggests that here is a universal truth. Each person individually experiences temptation; there is no exception. Further, each person is inescapably responsible, for temptation comes from "his own lust." Though there may be external promptings and allurements, temptation has its true source in inner lust. We may desire to excuse others' sinful behavior as the result of environment and external influences and pressures, but we dare not excuse ourselves for personal sin. Jesus taught that evil deeds come "out of the heart of men" (Mark 7:21); we cannot blame outward contamination. At the very beginning Adam blamed Eve, and Eve accused the serpent, but each was personally responsible. To flippantly

---

**New English Bible.*

say, "The devil made me do it," is to fail to face reality.

The Greek word for *lust* usually connotes evil, though at times it is used in a commendable way (1 Thess. 2:17, translated "desire"). In itself, it is a neutral word indicating strong desire. The individual has natural desires, such as the desire for food. Those desires are not bad in and of themselves; but when desires become inticements to do evil, such as to steal for food, then they become wrong. Eve had the desire for food, beauty, and wisdom—all normal desires—but Satan used those as contact points to lure Eve. In a similar manner John writes of "the lust of the flesh and the lust of the eyes and the boastful pride of life" (1 John 2:16).

The impulse toward sin was seen in Jewish theology as an evil impulse of *yeser.* The impulse itself was considered a simple, nondirected desire and a part of created human nature. But it was dangerous in that it could break the bounds of the law and therefore lead to sin. The solution was not the "removal of all desire, but a counterforce (variously described as the law, the good impulse, or the Holy Spirit) which channels and limits the evil impulse into doing good."[1] James's Jewish readers would be familiar with that concept.

Two participles, "carried away" and "enticed," are used to describe the method of operation used by lust. The first term is used of fishing and the second of both fishing and hunting. Both came to be used of the subtlety of the prostitute. "Carried away" comes from a Greek compound word meaning "to draw out." The imagery is that of bait's being used to beguile a fish out of its retreat, to lure it. Satan uses many different kinds of bait, and the impulses within are attracted to the bait. There is nothing wrong with the impulses, but the illicit use of those impulses can lead to sin and death. The fish's desire for food will cause it to be drawn away to the bait, which will lead to death. The desire for food is not

1. Peter H. Davids, *The Epistle of James, The New International Greek Commentary,* ed. I. Howard Marshall and W. Ward Gasque (Grand Rapids: Eerdmans, 1982), 36.

wrong, but if it leads to stealing for food it has become an instrument for evil that in turn will result in death.

The second term, "enticed," means "to trap with bait." It pictures the baiting of a trap or snare. The fish will see the worm or fly and its inner impulses will prompt it to bite. Immediately its anticipated pleasure turns to bitterness, for it has swallowed the bait, hook and all. Likewise the wild animal will be attracted to bait. If he takes it, suddenly he is ensnared. Allowing the attractions and allurements of sin to control our inner desires reaps a disastrous harvest.

The participles are both in the present tense; luring to sin is a continuing problem. The believer must always be on guard. The phrase "by his own lust" can be attached either to "tempted" or to "carried away and enticed." Is one tempted by his own lust, or is he carried away and enticed by his own lust? Although both are true, the imagery James is using argues for the second meaning. The bait attracts and stimulates the desires, resulting in temptation.

In this section James has not mentioned the activities of Satan (cf. 4:7). Rather than emphasizing the role of Satan in temptation, a concept clearly taught in Scripture (Luke 22:31; 1 Thess. 3:5; 1 Pet. 5:8), James is laying stress on the personal responsibility of each individual. Others are not to be blamed if one allows himself to be lured and baited.

The portrayal of allurement is continued in the imagery of the prostitute (v. 15). As the fisherman and hunter bait their prey, so also does the harlot. Solomon vividly portrayed the ensnaring activity of the woman of the night in Proverbs 7:6-23. He concludes:

> With her many persuasions she entices him;
> With her flattering lips she seduces him.
> Suddenly he follows her,
> As an ox goes to the slaughter,
> Or as one in fetters to the discipline of a fool,
> Until an arrow pierces through his liver;
> As a bird hastens to the snare,
> So he does not know that it will cost him his life.
> (vv. 21-23)

There is a sequence: desire, conception, birth, growth, and death. If the inner desire for the bait is repelled, conception and subsequent death will never take place. But if not, there is certain death. Solomon writes, "My son, if sinners entice you, do not consent" (Prov. 1:10). The sequence may also be seen as two births taking place: lust gives birth to sin, and sin gives birth to death.

Desire and sin must be distinguished. Man has certain desires; when those desires are responsive to temptation, they become lusts. When one's instinctive sexual desires are encouraged and yield to the enticements of the harlot, the resulting conception is sin. Lust is the mother of sin. "Sin" may be either understood as the sin nature, that inner dynamic in man that produces sinful acts (1 John 1:8), or as an overt act of sin (1 John 1:10). Here James is speaking of an act of sin. If an innocent and natural desire is allowed to germinate into lust, the result will be an act of sin. When the restraint of sinful desire is removed, all manner of evil is produced. Jeremiah wrote, "The heart is more deceitful than all else and is desperately sick; who can understand it?" (17:9). Our Lord taught that uncontrolled lust is sin, even as the act itself is (Matt. 5:28).

The first use of "sin" in verse 15 is without the article; the second occurrence has the article, referring to the particular sin just mentioned. The second occurrence might be better translated "that sin." If a certain sin is not cut short, that sin will reach full maturity; it will accomplish its full measure of evil, and the final consequence will be death. Sin becomes the mother of death, as lust is of sin. Adam and Eve responded to the bait of Satan and died. Paul wrote, "The wages of sin is death" (Rom. 6:23), and, "The mind set on the flesh is death" (Rom. 8:6).

"Death" means separation: separation from the body (physical death) or separation from God (spiritual death). No doubt James had in mind spiritual death. Isaiah contended, "But your iniquities have made a separation between you and your God, and your sins have hidden His face from you, so that He does not hear" (59:2). If spiritual death is not corrected by the One who can give life (John 10:10), it will result in eternal death. Rather than receiving the crown of life (v. 12), the sinner will receive death.

GOD BRINGS GOOD, NOT SIN (1:16-18)

Rather than accusing God of being the one who tempts with evil intentions, James reasons with his readers that they should see God as the source of good. There is both a sharpness and a tenderness in his appeal. On the one hand he commands them to stop being deceived; at the same time he addresses his readers as "my beloved brethren." This verse (v. 16) provides the transition between verses 13-14 and 17-18. James does not want them to be deceived about the true source of temptation and their responsibility in personal sin, nor does he want them to misunderstand that far from being the source of temptation, God is the wellspring of all good. "Deceived" is in the passive voice. The readers were being led astray. The negative suggests that they were to stop allowing themselves to be misled about this false concept of God and their own responsibility relative to temptation. Paul also uses that same command concerning false doctrine (1 Cor. 6:9; 15:33; Gal. 6:7).

James has used the address "my brethren" earlier (v. 2), but this is the first time he uses the fuller "my beloved brethren" (1:19; 2:5). There is a deep and loving brotherly concern that those in the Christian family not be led into error. That expression of tenderness from their Christian brother will motivate the readers to accept what is being taught.

Rather than envisioning God as a tempting, evil God, we must acknowledge Him as a giving, good God. That God is a giving God, introduced in verse 5, is now more fully developed. He is, in general, the source of every good thing (v. 17) and, in particular, the source of the good gift of regeneration (v. 18).

The two phrases "every good thing bestowed" and "every perfect gift" are in parallel construction. "Every" occurring at the start of each phrase emphasizes the comprehensiveness and inclusiveness of God's kindness. God alone is good in the absolute sense (Matt. 19:17), and He is the giver of good (Matt. 7:11) and (by implication) *only* good. The adjectives "good" and "perfect" emphasize two different concepts. The former suggests "useful, profitable, beneficial." "Perfect" emphasizes the gifts of God as being complete, lacking in nothing (cf. the use of the word in v. 4). Both "thing bestowed" and "gift" are built from the same verb meaning "to give." The first term emphasizes the act of giving, the endowment; the second term lays stress on the gift. God's giving is good in the sense of being beneficial, and the gift is perfect in the sense of being complete, without lack.

Translations will vary on the position of "is." The rendering may be, "Every perfect gift is from above, coming down . . . ," or, "Every perfect gift from above is coming down." In either case, the meaning is much the same. "From above" reminds the reader of the heavenly source of all good things. The believer has been born from above (John 3:7), Christ came from above (John 3:31), and the believer is to seek those things above (Col. 3:1). Later James contrasts the wisdom that comes from above with that which is earthly, natural, and demonic (3:13-18). "Coming down" is a present tense participle. The gifts are portrayed as continually coming down from above in a never-ending stream.

The fountainhead of those gifts is "the Father of lights." *Light* is used in Scripture in many ways: physical light (Gen. 1:3; 2 Cor. 4:6); luminaries, such as the sun, moon, or stars (Gen. 1:14-18; John 11:9); the nature of God (1 John 1:7); saving or divine truth (John 1:4; 1 John 2:8); reason or power of understanding (Luke 11:34-35); and spiritual purity as opposed to darkness (2 Cor. 6:14; Eph. 5:8). Here the term is plural and has the article, indicating that it has reference to the heavenly luminaries of the physical universe. "Father" can be used of God both in a creative and redemptive sense. He is the Father of creation because He is the Creator (Job 38:28; Mal. 2:10; Eph. 3:15). He is the one "who made the great lights'' (Ps. 136:7). God is also the Father in a redemptive sense, the Father of those who believe (Matt. 6:9; Rom. 8:15; 1 John 3:1). The use of ''Father'' prepares the readers for the imagery of the new birth introduced in the next verse.

The lights of the firmament, established by God for signs, seasons, days, and years (Gen. 1:14), follow perfectly their God-ordained orbits. As the earth turns on its axis and rotates around the sun, moving shadows are cast and the heavenly bodies appear to shift about in the firmament. James uses that physical phenomenon in contrast to the immutable God. There is with the Creator of those lights ''no variation, or shifting shadow.'' ''Variation,'' a term occurring only here in the New Testament, denotes the constant change among the heavenly bodies. There is the variation of light between the sun and the moon and between the stars, changes in the length of daylight during the four seasons of the year, the shifting positions of the rising and setting sun throughout the year, and the change in the light from the sun or moon from one hour to the next. In contrast to those lights, the one who is light never changes. He is the eternal, immutable fountainhead of light.

Further, with Him there is no ''shifting shadow.'' There are some differences among the Greek manuscripts and translations concerning the exact rendering of that expression. The following are examples: ''No play of passing shadows'' (NEB), ''shadow that is cast by turning'' (ASV*), ''shadow due to change'' (RSV†), ''shadow of turning'' (KJV‡), and ''shifting shadows'' (NIV§). Shadows are formed when the sun or moon has been eclipsed by some object, such as a tree or building; and as the earth rotates, those shadows move. When one is behind the shadow he is hindered from seeing the source of the light. Two truths about God can be derived from James's imagery: God is never eclipsed, and His

---

**American Standard Version.*
†*Revised Standard Version.*
‡*King James Version.*
§*New International Version.*

light is unvarying, consistent, and uniform. John writes, "God is light, and in Him there is no darkness at all" (1 John 1:5).

One of the good gifts of God is the new birth (v. 18). "So far from God tempting us to evil, His will is the cause of our regeneration."[2] God was good in creating the heavenly lights, but how much better in giving spiritual light. Man was created in the image of God (Gen. 1:26-27; 2:7), and at salvation he is "born again to a living hope" (1 Pet. 1:3). The new birth is accomplished "in the exercise of His will." John writes that believers are "born not of blood, nor of the will of the flesh, nor of the will of man, but of God" (John 1:13). That is reminiscent of the words of our Lord "You did not choose Me, but I chose you" (John 15:16). He did not will our condemnation (2 Pet. 3:9) but our salvation.

"Brought us forth" is the same verb as that used in verse 15. Sin brings forth death, but God brings forth life. Both "will" and "brought forth" are in the aorist tense; having willed our new birth, God at a point in time caused us to be born again. The means of our regeneration is "the word of truth." Peter declared that the believer is born again "through the living and abiding word of God" (1 Pet. 1:23), and then he wrote that the Word of God is "the word which was preached" (1 Pet. 1:25). Of the Thessalonians Paul wrote, "When you received from us the word of God's message, you accepted it . . . [as] the word of God, which also performs its work in you who believe" (1 Thess. 2:13). When faithfully proclaimed in the power of the Spirit, the gospel message will bear fruit and effect regeneration (Rom. 10:17).

Our regeneration has a goal: "so that we might be, as it were, the first fruits among His creatures." "First fruits" has its setting in the Old Testament Levitical system. The Jewish readers would be reminded of that first portion of the harvest, which belonged to God (Lev. 10-11). It was not only

2. Mayor, 62.

to be the firstfruits in terms of time, the first of the harvest, but also in quality, "*choice* first fruits" (Ex. 23:19, italics added). Christ is "the first fruits" of the resurrection (1 Cor. 15:23). The believer has "the first fruits of the Spirit" (Rom. 8:23), as a foretaste of what is yet to come. The figure was used by Paul to speak of the first converts in an area as representative of those who would yet come to faith and be a part of the larger harvest (Rom. 16:5; 1 Cor. 16:15). James's Jewish readers could identify with the metaphor in several ways. In point of time the gospel did come to the Jew first; they were the firstfruits (Rom. 1:16). Looking at it from the standpoint of church history, surely the early church was the firstfruits. And further, from the standpoint of priority and quality, the people of God are the chief of God's creation. The phrase "His creatures" embraces not only Christians but all mankind, and more than that, all of God's creatures, though the emphasis is primarily on mankind.

The believer is a new creature in Christ. He has been recreated into the image of Him who created him (Eph. 4:24; Col. 3:10). Paul writes, "As we have borne the image of the earthly, we shall also bear the image of the heavenly" (1 Cor. 15:49). Far from God enticing us to evil, He provides good things. He has brought salvation and made us firstfruits of His creatures.

3

USING THE WORD FOR SPIRITUAL MATURING

JAMES 1:19-27

The mention of regeneration through the Word (v. 18) fittingly introduces new thoughts concerning the Word. As the Word produces regeneration, so it is also a means of sanctification. After writing of the experience of the new birth, James continues with the challenge to live out the new life by means of the Word. These nine verses can be divided into three sections: the reception of the Word (vv. 19-21), the doing of the Word (vv. 22-25), and the application of the Word (vv. 26-27).

THE RECEPTION OF THE WORD (1:19-21)

Greek manuscripts vary on the first word. Some read "wherefore" (*hoste*); others read "you know" (*iste*). The latter reading is followed uniformly by modern translations, though they differ in its rendering. It may be understood as imperative, "know this," or as indicative, "you know." If it is taken as an imperative, it would naturally go with what follows and would read, "My dear brothers, take note of this: Everyone should be quick . . ." (NIV). On the other hand, if it is understood as an indicative, it goes with what came before. The readers knew that they had been regenerated by the Word and were firstfruits. James could now proceed with certain commands in light of what they knew about their redemption.

By the use of the full "my beloved brethren," the author

appeals to them as fellow family members, objects of his brotherly concern (cf. vv. 2, 16). That prepares the way for the threefold admonition "Be quick to hear, slow to speak, and slow to anger." Each of these subjects is discussed later at greater length: "quick to hear" (1:22-25), "slow to speak" (3:1-12), and "slow to anger" (3:13-18).

The appeal is made to "every one." Each individual Christian, with no exception, struggles with the control of the tongue. The present tenses indicate that it is a continuing problem. Proverbs gives counsel similar to James's: "When there are many words, trangression is unavoidable, but he who restrains his lips is wise" (Prov. 10:19); and, "He who is slow to anger is better than the mighty, and he who rules his spirit, than he who captures a city" (Prov. 16:32; see also 13:3; 18:13). An ancient rabbinical parallel is, "Even a fool, as long as he keeps silent, is regarded as wise."[1]

If this threefold admonition is addressed primarily to preachers and teachers, the command is that they be careful to be attentive to the voice of God and careful to give forth truth that comes from God. The teacher must be careful not to speak on his own initiative or with a hasty response; he must first be tuned into and responsive to the Word, meditating on it. Then he will be prepared to communicate it to others. The communicator of truth may sometimes face criticism or opposition, but he must not respond in anger.

Since the command is addressed to "every one" though, it is probably better to understand it as a responsibility of every Christian. All Christians, regardless of their maturity in the faith or position in the church, should be ready to listen to God's revealed truth, not reacting rashly or rushing impatiently to communicate it to others before they have thought it through and allowed it to work in their own lives.

Listening is the first duty of discipleship, so the first challenge is to be "quick to hear." That implies both the public and private reading of Scripture as well as the public

---

1. Hiebert, 124.

instruction of the teachers. When James wrote, none of the New Testament was available. The canon was limited to the Old Testament (1 Tim. 4:13; 2 Tim. 3:15; 4:2), and his Jewish readers would be familir with it. As the apostles spoke and wrote in the power of the Holy Spirit, their communications were also to be accepted as the Word of God (1 Thess. 2:13; 2 Thess. 2:15). This letter from James was to be accepted as a message from God, and the readers were to be "swift to hear" it as well as the rest of Scripture. Today the complete Scripture, consisting of the Old and New Testaments, is available. In addition, God has provided to each believer His Holy Spirit to enable the believer to interpret and apply it correctly (John 14:26; 16:13; 1 John 2:20, 27). God has also placed in the local church pastors and teachers to be used of Him in leading the church toward maturity (Eph. 4:11-13).

There is always a danger in speaking too quickly. A rabbi writes, "Speech for a shekel, silence for two; it is like a precious stone."[2] The apocryphal book Ecclesiasticus states: "Be quick to listen, but take time over your answer. Answer a man if you know what to say, but if not, hold your tongue" (5:11, NEB). The early church service was probably not structured in a formal way, and the assembly had considerable audience participation (1 Cor. 14:26-33). It would be easy to stir up controversy with rash and hasty response. The listener is to listen attentively to the reading of Scripture and the message, analyzing the arguments and explanations, then if he must respond, he should do so thoughtfully, deliberately, and courteously. Jesus often warned His hearers about impetuous speech (Matt. 5:37; 7:1; 12:36-37; Luke 6:45; cf. Eph. 4:26; Col. 4:6).

Reckless speech can lead to and engender anger, so the believer is commanded to be "slow to anger." That is not to be understood as the quick outburst of wrath, but rather the persistent and strong feeling of resentment, the harboring of

---

2. W. E. Oesterley, "The General Epistle of James," *The Expositor's Greek Testament,* ed. W. Robertson Nicoll (Grand Rapids: Eerdmans, 1951), 4:431.

animosity toward a brother or sister. To be sure, the Christian must be angry with sin (see Mark 3:5), but even then the anger must be controlled (Eph. 4:26). Nowhere does Scripture permit the venting of personal vengeance. Heated discussion can often lead to animosity and feelings of resentment. That the believer must avoid.

The reason to avoid wrath is because man's wrath does not advance the work of God (v. 20). "The anger of man" stands in marked contrast to "the righteousness of God." *Righteousness* is a broad word in Scripture. It may speak of being right with God in the sense of being declared righteous, being justified; or it may mean doing right things, being just and equitable. In Paul's epistles the first meaning is predominant, but James uses "righteous" and "righteousness" to describe conduct that is right (3:18; 5:6, 16). Right actions are the product of being justified.

"Achieve" may mean that man's wrath does not do what is right in the sight of God, or that man's wrath does not further righteousness. Both ideas are true. Nothing that is right in the sight of God is furthered or performed by human anger. Though there is righteous anger, wild and uncontrolled human anger will never bring about righteous actions. What God requires of a man is that he "do justice" (Mic. 6:8).

"Therefore" (v. 21) indicates an inference that can be drawn from verse 20. Rather than responding in anger, the Christian should do two things: first, strip off the vestiges of the old life; and then, welcome the Word with its life-changing power. Two metaphors are used: the first relates to the putting off of clothing, and the second, "implanted," is derived from farming.

The relationship of the participle "putting aside" to the imperative "receive" suggests that the "putting aside" is antecedent to the receiving. The believer must first put off certain things; then he can receive. The metaphor of taking off clothing is used often in Scripture to portray the removal of unbecoming traits related to the old life (Rom. 13:12; Eph.

4:22). The writer to the Hebrews uses it of stripping for a race (Heb. 12:1). Peter also uses the concept in his discussion of the reception of the Word (1 Pet. 2:1). Two items are to be laid aside: "all filthiness and all that remains of wickedness." "Filthiness," used of dirty clothing (cf. 2:2), continues the metaphor. "All" should be taken comprehensively; all kinds of filthiness as well as each individual aspect of filthiness must be removed. God wants His followers to be morally pure and unsoiled in all areas of life. In the symbolic act of Zechariah 3:4, the removal of Joshua's filthy garments portrayed the removal of his iniquity.

The "remains of wickedness" are also to be removed. That phrase has been understood in different ways. *Wickedness* may have the general meaning of evil, vice, or depravity as opposed to virtue; or it may mean the more specific malice or ill will (cf. 1 Pet. 2:1). Further, *all that remains* may carry the idea of residue, that which is left over, or it may mean overabundance (cf. Rom. 5:17). Because of those various possibilities, the phrase has been variously translated: "overflowing of wickedness" (ASV), "the malice that hurries to excess" (NEB), "superfluity of naughtiness" (KJV), "rank growth of wickedness" (RSV), "the evil that is so prevalent" (NIV). James is calling upon his readers to strip off all that is left of wickedness.

The negative "putting aside" is balanced with the positive "receive," a term that includes the concept of welcoming (Matt. 10:40; Gal. 4:14; Heb. 11:31). What is to be received is the "word implanted." Through the Word, regeneration has taken place (v. 18). For growth to take place, the soil must be hospitable to the seed; it must welcome the implanted seed of the Word. Perhaps James had in mind the parable of the sower (Matt. 13:3-9, 18-23) in which the productivity of the seeds was dependent upon the receptivity and condition of the soil. The Word is to be received with "humility," meaning "mildness, gentleness." Rather than being self-assertive and brash, the true believer should receive with gentleness and consideration the Word. He should be ready and eager to learn and respond gladly to the will of God as shown in His Word (1 Pet. 2:1-2).

The implanted Word "is able to save" the soul. The term *save* has an eschatological meaning here, as it does in 4:12 and 5:20: salvation from eternal death. There is a sense in which a believer is saved at the point of conversion (Eph. 2:8), and there is also a sense in which a believer is being saved as he grows and matures in this life (1 Cor. 1:18). James emphasizes final salvation, which occurs at the return of Christ. The Word regenerates (v. 18), sanctifies (v. 19; cf. John 17:17), and provides ultimate salvation (v. 21).

The "soul" is that which is saved. It may refer to the whole person (John 10:15; Acts 2:41), or the immaterial part of man as distinct from the material (Matt. 10:28; Rev. 6:9). Here, no doubt, James is considering the whole person. Final and complete salvation involves body and soul.

THE DOING OF THE WORD (1:22-25)

Having received the Word, there is now an obligation to do it. Hearing is a necessary part of the Christian experience (Acts 15:7; Rom. 10:14; Eph. 1:13), but it must go beyond that to action. As hearing must be united with faith to be effective (Heb. 4:2), so it must also result in doing. In the parable of the two foundations (Matt. 7:24-27), the man who built on the sand was the hearer only, and the one who built on the rock was both a hearer and a doer of Jesus' words. Jesus said, "Blessed are those who hear the word of God, and observe it" (Luke 11:28; cf. Rev. 1:3; 22:7). Paul argued that it was not the hearers of the law who were justified, but the doers (Rom. 2:13). It is not sufficient to hear the message; one must act upon it. "Delude," not the same term translated "deceived" (v. 16), refers to irrational or fallacious reasoning. It is in the middle voice, suggesting that those who were hearers only were rationalizing their pious inaction. True Christianity must move from the pew to the marketplace.

James illustrates his point by an example of wrong and right behavior. The first example is of the wrong behavior: listening but not doing (vv. 23-24). The portrait is of one who looks into a mirror and leaves without making any changes in his appearance, forgetting what he saw. "Natural face" is the face of one's birth, the physical face.

Three actions continue the illustration (v. 24). The first and last verbs are aorists, and the middle one is a perfect. He looks, then goes away and forgets. "Gone away" is in the perfect tense, emphasizing a continuing and sustained state. The picture then is of one who merely looks at himself in the mirror, does not take the time to make necessary improvements in his appearance and correct such things as a smudged face or disheveled hair, but quickly moves on, forgetting what he saw. For a second time James has drawn attention to the fleeting nature of human existence (see v. 11).

In sharp contrast to the illustration of the hearer only is that of the one who also is a doer of the Word (v. 25). James does not continue the metaphor of the mirror but rather moves into reality. The mirror is the perfect law into which the believer must look. "Looks intently" is a word picture of one bending over to get a closer look. It is the word used by John to describe how John and Mary peered into the empty tomb (John 20:5, 11). It is also used of angels who long "to look" into the salvation provided by Christ (1 Pet. 1:12). Here then is a picture of one bending over the perfect law to make careful examination, in contrast to the careless hearer illustrated by the hasty glance in the mirror. "The perfect law," explained as "the law of liberty," was mentioned earlier as "the word of truth" (v. 18) and "the word" (v. 21). Paul calls it "the law of Christ" (1 Cor. 9:21; Gal. 6:2) and "the law of faith" (Rom. 3:27). "Law" is used without the article, suggesting nature and quality. It is the body of truth, the standard by which the Christian life is lived and regulated. It is the spirit of the law as interpreted by Jesus Christ and more fully elaborated by the apostles in the New Testament. The law is qualified by two terms: *perfect* and *liberty*. It is perfect in the sense that it is final and complete. It gives the full picture of God's character and righteousness and summarizes God's just precepts into two all-encompassing demands: a thoroughgoing love for God and neighbor (Mark 12:30-31; Luke 10:27; Gal. 5:14). James later identifies the love for neighbor as "the royal law" (2:8).

The law is also called the law of "liberty" (see 2:12). The word *liberty* has the article, pointing to the well-known liberty found in Christ. Both sin and legalism enslave, but the law of Christ promises freedom (John 8:32-36; 2 Cor. 3:17; Gal. 5:1). Christians are made free from the law (Rom. 7:3) and sin (Rom. 6:20). Paul wrote, "For the law of the Spirit of life in Christ Jesus has set you free from the law of sin and of death" (Rom. 8:2). One of the benefits of the new covenant in which the church shares is the law of God within, written on the heart (2 Cor. 3:3; cf. Jer. 31:33). The concept of the law written in the heart parallels the "implanted" Word mentioned earlier (1:21).

This new freedom in Christ is not antinomian; it is "the law" of liberty. Though the term itself is not repeated, the use of the article makes the designation clear. Christian liberty is not freedom from all bonds; it does not free one from accountability. Paul writes, "For you were called to freedom, brethren; only do not turn your freedom into an opportunity for the flesh, but through love serve one another" (Gal. 5:13), and in a similar vein Peter encourages his readers, "Act as free men, and do not use your freedom as a covering for evil, but use it as bondslaves of God" (1 Pet. 2:16).

The one who stoops to look intently at the Word and continues doing so has become not a "forgetful hearer but an effectual doer." In the original the double description is parallel: "hearer of forgetfulness" and "doer of work." The "non-doer" of verses 23-24 was also a "forgetter." The true disciple must be one who hears the Word, does not forget it, and does it.

Earlier, blessedness was ascribed to the one who perseveres (v. 12); now the same pronouncement is given to the one who is a faithful doer. That is reminiscent of what Jesus said, "If you know these things, you are blessed if you do them" (John 13:17). He had earlier declared, "Blessed are those who hear the word of God, and observe it" (Luke 11:28). "What he does" is literally "in his doing." It speaks of a person's whole life-style, not merely isolated actions. Having challenged the readers to receive the Word and then do it, James now proceeds to give clear examples of doing the Word.

THE APPLICATION OF THE WORD (1:26-27)

The application of the Word is approached from a negative standpoint, then a positive. There is on the one hand a need for a bridled tongue, and on the other the need for positive Christian action motivated by a pure heart.

"If" introduces another example of self-deception (v. 26; cf. 1:16, 22). The clause "If any one thinks himself to be religious" may be rendered, "If any man among you seem to be religious" (KJV). The meaning would emphasize the public appearance or outside reputation. That meaning can be rejected, though, because the controlled tongue would negate whatever thoughts there might be about being genuinely religious. Instead, the meaning followed by most translations is that of self-deception; one imagines himself to be religious. The adjective *religious* occurs only here in the New Testament, whereas the noun form, *religion,* is found later in this verse and in verse 27 (see also Acts 26:5; Col. 2:23). Jesus commented on the outward forms of religion when He spoke of fasting, public praying, and almsgiving (Matt. 6:1-18). The Old Testament prophets often called upon the people to make their faith more than mere form. The Lord said, "For I delight in loyalty rather than sacrifice, and in the knowledge of God rather than burnt offerings" (Hos. 6:6; cf. Isa. 58:5; Mic. 6:6-8; Matt. 9:13). The broken spirit and contrite heart must come before the offering of sacrifices (Ps. 51:16-19).

One sign of genuine religion is a bridled tongue. It is self-deception for one to claim to be religious when the tongue has not been bridled. The participle translated "bridle," used again in 3:2, is a compound form meaning "to lead with a bridle." The tongue is likened to an unruly horse that needs a bit and bridle to bring it under control. The tongue is an exceedingly powerful instrument that can be used for good or ill. The Christian is challenged to control the tongue, using it for good. His speech is to be "with grace, seasoned, as it were, with salt" (Col. 4:6). Solomon wrote, "He who guards his mouth and his tongue, guards his soul from troubles" (Prov. 21:23). To claim a true form of religion yet not control the tongue is to have a "worthless" religion. *Worthless,* sometimes translated "vain," means "unprofitable" (cf. 1 Cor. 15:17; Titus 3:9). Outward forms of religion are useless without the inner dynamic of the Holy Spirit.

True religion is more than form worship; it must have an effect on one's life-style (v. 27). Piety and purity go together. Two important areas in religion are mentioned: genuine concern for the needy and the need for personal purity. What God wants is "pure and undefiled religion." Though the terms may be used in a ceremonial sense, James uses them in an ethical, moral sense. "Pure" means "to be free from anything that soils; to be chaste, clean." "Undefiled" is the negative form of the word meaning "stained, polluted, soiled." What God wants is a religion that is chaste and unsoiled. Moral cleanness is more important than ceremonial cleanness. Religious acts may impress man, but true religion must hold up in the presence of God. He will be the final judge, and it is ultimately before Him that we stand or fall (Rom. 14:4). "God and Father" is a distinctive Christian formula (Gal. 1:4; Eph. 1:3); "God" emphasizes His authority, and "Father" reminds the reader of a family relationship. Because our lives are spent in the presence of God, who is indeed our Father, we dare not be hypocritical in our religious exercise.

One true act of religious service is "to visit orphans and widows in their distress." One does not read far in Scripture before recognizing that there is a special place in the heart of God for the afflicted. God is "a father of the fatherless and a judge for the widows" (Psalm 68:5). The law says, "Cursed is he who distorts the justice due an alien, orphan, and widow" (Deut. 27:19; cf. Ex. 22:22). A priority in the family of God is to care for those who are needy. Jesus cared for the widow of Nain (Luke 7:12-15), the early church appointed administrators to care for the neglected widows (Acts 6:1-6), and deserving needy widows were put on the list for material benefit (1 Tim. 5:3-16). "Distress" probably refers to their physical plight. A fatherless home needs the loving support of the Christian community.

True religion is "to visit" such people. That denotes more than the mere paying of a social visit or the impersonal giving of funds through an agency; it is that personal coming to the aid of a needy individual. The same verb was used twice by Jesus when He gave the parable of the sheep and the goats (Matt. 25:36, 43). In place of mere religious rite, Paul emphasized that Christian behavior was "faith working through love" (Gal. 5:6).

Another side of true religion is "to keep oneself unstained by the world." Though not of the world, the Christian is in the world (John 17:11, 14), and the whole world lies in the evil one (1 John 5:19; cf. John 17:15). The world is, in this case, not the created material world, but the moral world—that mass of unredeemed mankind who are enemies of God and His purposes. It is the world system controlled by "the prince of the power of the air" (Eph. 2:2), the one called "the ruler of the world" (John 14:30). Later James writes that "friendship with the world is hostility toward God" (4:4). The Christian should not, nor can he, isolate himself from the world (1 Cor. 5:9-11), but he dare not let its demoralizing influence impact his personal purity. Paul admonished Timothy, "Keep yourself free [pure] from sin" (1 Tim. 5:22).

Though ultimately it is God who keeps (1 Thess. 5:23), there is also the individual responsibility to keep oneself pure (1 Pet. 1:15-16). The true believer will persevere, and at His return Christ shall "present to Himself the church in all her glory, having no spot or wrinkle or any such thing'' (Eph. 5:27).

Those outward demonstrations of true faith should not be construed to replace the inner need for a changed heart, but the inner change will manifest itself in a godly life-style. The Word of God transforms the life within and without.

4

ACCEPTING OTHERS WITHOUT PARTIALITY

JAMES 2:1-13

The first paragraph of James 2 relates to the preceding chapter in two ways. It continues the discussion of true religion (1:26-27). As godly behavior will express itself in a sympathetic attitude toward the disenfranchised and in a separation from sinful behavior, so it will also demonstrate itself in an accepting, nonprejudicial attitude toward the poor and the societal outcast. This section also continues the earlier emphasis on the democracy or equality of faith (1:9-11).

The subject of prejudicial behavior is introduced in verse 1, then it is rejected along three lines: prejudice is a result of evil motives (2:2-4), it is inconsistent with loving one another (2:5-9), and it is judging without proper mercy (2:10-13).

"My brethren" introduces a new section and once again subtly reminds the readers that the church is a family (cf. 1:2, 9, 16, 19). Evidently there was a lack of love and brotherhood in the church, and that needed to be addressed. The verse may be understood as imperative, "Do not hold your faith . . . ," or as a question, "Do you hold your faith . . . ?" Most translations agree that it should be rendered as an imperative, a prohibition against partiality in the Christian community. "Hold your faith in" is confessional. It is inconsistent for those who confess to have faith in Jesus and who acknowledge His lordship to fail in their acceptance of others.

The meaning of "glorious" is a disputed issue. The literal rendering is "our Lord Jesus Christ the glory." Some translations make it adjectival, "our glorious Lord Jesus Christ" (NASB, NIV); others prefer to add "the Lord," rendering the phrase "our Lord Jesus Christ the Lord of glory" (KJV, RSV). Perhaps it is best taken as appositional to Jesus Christ; He is the glory. In the back of James's mind may have been the Shekinah, the glory dwelling with man (Ex. 13:21-22; Lev. 26:11; Zech. 2:5; Rev. 21:3). Jesus showed forth the divine glory in the days of His flesh (John 1:14; 2:11; 2 Cor. 4:6; Heb. 1:3), and in His resurrection and ascension (John 17:1, 5). That the God of glory became man should humble and disarm anyone who would entertain the thought of class prejudice in the church (Phil. 2:5-8). Neither the Old Testament (Lev. 19:15) nor the New Testament (Acts 10:34) allow for such behavior. Peter had addressed the Jerusalem Council, moderated by James, about another type of prejudice, racial prejudice. Concerning the free gift of salvation he said, "He [God] made no distinction between us [Jews] and them [Gentiles], cleansing their hearts by faith" (Acts 15:9).

PREJUDICE IS A RESULT OF EVIL MOTIVES (2:2-4)

After the introductory injunction, James gives a vivid, hypothetical illustration of partiality that his readers would readily understand. Two visitors, probably non-believers, enter the worship meeting, one shortly after the other (note the repeated use of "comes"). One of the visitors is rich, the other poor, as evidenced by their garments. How the two are treated becomes a test of true Christian faith.

That James is speaking of the public assembly for worship is clear from his use of the word "assembly" (*sunagōgēn,* lit. "synagogue"). That is the common New Testament term for the Jewish place of worship (Mark 6:2; Acts 14:1). The early church service and polity was patterned to a large extent after the synagogue; prayer, Scripture reading, and preaching were all a part of the service (Luke 4:16-21; 13:10-15; 1 Tim. 4:13). It was natural for a group of Jewish believers to call their worship assembly a synagogue. That fact suggests a relatively early date for the epistle, a time when the terms *synagogue* and *church* were used interchangeably (5:14). Because the meetings were public (1 Cor. 14:23-25) it is easy to visualize the two, the rich man and the poor man, entering as visitors into the gathering.

There is a vivid contrast in their appearance. The wealthy man has a "gold ring" (lit., "gold-fingered," meaning "many gold rings") and "fine clothes." "Fine" is literally "bright, sparkling" (cf. Acts 10:30). The picture suggests a wealthy Jew entering with an air of pomp and ostentatiousness, though the point of the illustration is not the attitude of the visitors but that of the assembly toward the visitors. In sharp contrast to the rich man is the "poor man in dirty clothes." Rather than gold rings and sparkling clothing, his are shabby and work-stained. In the Christian community both should be equally accepted, for God is no respecter of persons; but the temptation is to give special recognition to the more "respectable" of the two.

Verse 3 moves from the entrance of the visitors to the hypothetical reaction of the believing community. "You" is in the plural, indicating the general attitude of the group. Prejudice is a cancer that has permeated the whole body. "Pay special attention" is from the verb "look upon," and in this case "look upon with favor." The group is awed by the appearance of the smartly dressed man and requests him to sit in a privileged place.

The exact meaning of "good" (*kalōs*) in this context is not certain. It may refer to a good place or seat (NASB), or it may be understood as "please," an indication of courteous and special treatment (RSV). Probably it is best to understand it as referring to an especially comfortable seat in an imposing location.

The poor man is rather carelessly treated. He may either stand, or if necessary sit on the floor. Not only is the poor visitor being treated worse than the rich one, he is also being treated as inferior to a regular communicant. He should have at least been offered one of their seats. The two visitors were judged by external criteria and not according to their true character and worth. Church members who were bearing the name of Christ were doing something that God Himself would not do, for with God there is no partiality (Rom. 2:11; Eph. 6:9; 1 Pet. 1:17).

There are two things wrong with the behavior portrayed: unnecessary distinctions were being made between the visitors, and there was evil thinking in those making those judgments (v. 4). The verb "made distinctions" can refer to inner turmoil in the sense of doubting or being double-minded (cf. 1:6), or to external judging between parties, making class distinctions. If it is the former meaning, then "among yourselves" would refer to the inner double-mindedness and turmoil within oneself about accepting or rejecting a person; they were doubting within themselves. If the second meaning is adopted, it speaks of the assembly's making class distinctions within itself. The second view seems the more appropriate in light of the context.

An interesting play on words is made at this point. Those making distinctions (*diekrithēte;* lit., "judge between") were becoming "judges" (*kritai*). Later James writes of one who speaks against a fellow believer as a "judge" (4:11). To judge by outward appearance is contrary to the biblical method, for God looks on the heart (1 Sam. 16:7). In the future, Christ will not judge by what He sees or hears, but He will judge with righteousness and fairness (Isa. 11:3-4). Prejudicial judging springs from "evil motives." "Motives" is the word *reasonings* (cf. Luke 5:21-22); "evil motives" are those reasonings that are injurious or destructive. Jesus used those words when He said, "For out of the heart come evil thoughts" (Matt. 15:19). That reflects a fundamental problem in the assembly. Judgment must not be made solely on external grounds. It is injurious to the individual being judged and has a negative effect on the whole body.

Some have conjectured that the setting portrayed by James is not actually a regular worship service in which partiality is being shown, but a church court, perhaps patterned after the Jewish synagogue's *beth-din.* Davids suggests, "The assembly is a judicial assembly of the church and both litigants are strangers to the process."[1] That idea is argued along several lines: the participants appear not to know each other; they seem to be strangers to the court and need special seating instructions; further, the judging taking place is judicial partiality, a partiality described in some of the rabbinical writings. Whether James is portraying a church court or (more probably) the regular worship service of the assembly, the point is the same: Christians should have no part in prejudicial judging, be it formal or informal.

PREJUDICE IS INCONSISTENT WITH LOVING ONE ANOTHER (2:5-9)

In a passionate appeal, James continues his argument against partiality along several lines. He reasons that God has chosen the poor to be rich in faith (v. 5), and that as a matter of historical record it is the rich who oppress (vv. 6-7). It is hardly proper to honor those who have traditionally been oppressors of the poor, while at the same time to dishonor those who are poor. The heart of the law demands love, and partiality is sin, not love (vv. 8-9).

"Listen" (v. 5) is an impassioned plea to the readers, as if James were actually speaking to them (cf. 1:16; 4:13; Acts 15:13). The use of "my beloved brethren" again assures the readers of his loving family relationship to them (1:16, 19) and his concern for the welfare of the brotherhood, the family of God. The inconsistency of partiality and prejudice between the materially rich and poor is shown to be twofold: first, God has chosen the poor to be rich in faith; and second, the actions of the rich toward the poor show them to be undeserving of being singled out for preferred treatment. "The rich" and "the poor" must be understood as general representative terms, for clearly there are exceptions. The poor are not automatically to be understood as righteous, nor the rich as unrighteous. James is presenting what is generally understood to be the case.

---

1. Davids, 109.

The gospel has always made a strong appeal to those who are poor in earthly goods. That the gospel was to be preached to the underprivileged was a part of the messianic role (Isa. 61:1-2). Jesus Himself used that prediction to authenticate His message (Luke 4:18; 7:22). It is the foolish, the weak, the base, and the despised whom God has chosen (1 Cor. 1:26-29). Jesus said, "Blessed are the poor in spirit, for theirs is the kingdom of heaven" (Matt. 5:3; cf. Luke 6:20). "Choose" indicates the poor are objects of God's special favor. That is reminiscent of God's choice of Israel. He chose Israel, not because they were many, but because He loved them (Deut. 7:6-8). That should not be construed to mean that all the poor will be saved, nor does it mean that there is anything meritorious in poverty; but it does affirm that the poor are not at a disadvantage to accept the salvation provided by the Lord. It vividly demonstrates that those so often rejected by man have been chosen by God. To be chosen by God is a gracious truth found throughout Scripture (Rom. 8:33; Eph. 1:4; 2 Thess. 2:13; 1 Pet. 1:1-2).

"Rich in faith" refers to spiritual riches, salvation with all of its accompanying blessings. Christ speaks of "true" wealth (Luke 16:11), "treasures in heaven" (Matt. 6:20), and being "rich toward God" (Luke 12:21). Part of that wealth is being "heirs of the kingdom." Jesus said, "Do not be afraid, little flock, for your Father has chosen gladly to give you the kingdom. Sell your possessions and give to charity; make yourselves purses which do not wear out, an unfailing treasure in heaven, where no thief comes near, nor moth destroys" (Luke 12:32-33). He also reflected, "How hard it is for those who are wealthy to enter the kingdom of God!" (Luke 18:24).

James views the kingdom as yet future, as eschatological. Although it is true that there is a sense in which the kingdom is present in the hearts and lives of those who believe (Rom. 14:17; cf. John 3:5), the full manifestation of it will not appear until Christ returns in glory. In that day heirs of the kingdom will reign with Christ (Matt. 19:28-30; 2 Tim. 2:12;

Rev. 2:26-27). Inheriting the kingdom is an important theme of Scripture (1 Cor. 6:9-10; 15:50; Gal. 5:21; Eph. 5:5; cf. Heb. 6:12; 1 Pet. 3:9). Those who will inherit the kingdom are "those who love Him." Those who love Him were earlier promised the crown of life (1:12). The promise of heirship goes back as far as Abraham; by faith in the promise he became an heir (Rom. 4:13-14; Gal. 3:18).

The poor who are potential heirs of the kingdom, though, are being dishonored by kingdom citizens (v. 6). Those whom God has chosen they have dishonored. The emphatic "you" is plural, suggesting an indictment against the whole group. Prejudice is a cancer that can permeate the whole body.

James proceeds to remind his readers by the use of two questions, both assuming an affirmative answer, that the rich have not shown themselves to be deserving of special treatment. The first question relates to daily life (v. 6), and the second to their religious hostility (v. 7). In their daily experience those Christians had encountered two hostile actions of the rich: personal oppression and the initiation of legal procedures against them. Some of those oppressive acts are mentioned by James later (5:1-6). Other examples of oppression by the rich are given in Acts. Certain Philippians dragged Paul and Silas to the authorities because "their hope of profit was gone" (Acts 16:19). When those of Ephesus turned to the Lord from serving Artemis (Diana), the silversmiths were greatly disturbed that their trade would "fall into disrepute" (19:27). Paul himself, before his conversion, actively persecuted the church (8:3, 22:4), even forcing those persecuted to blaspheme (26:11). That those poor people were being arrested and dragged into court suggests that the rich were seeking "to rob the Christians 'legally' of what was rightfully theirs"[2] through fabricated charges (cf. Acts 6:13; 21:28; Heb. 10:32-34). Those persecutions were all in keeping with what Jesus predicted (Matt. 10:17-23).

Not only did the rich engage in oppressive hostility against

2. Ibid., 113.

the Christians, they also spoke with contempt against the One whom the Christians loved and served. They blasphemed "the fair name" (v. 7). No doubt James had in mind the name of Jesus. The early church often referred to Jesus as "the Name" (3 John 7; cf. Acts 5:41; 15:14). It is the name above every name (Phil. 2:9), the name that has the power to save (Acts 4:12). Peter writes of believers being "reviled for the name of Christ" (1 Pet. 4:14), and suffering "as a Christian" (1 Pet. 4:16). It is a "fair" (*kalon,* meaning "honorable," beautiful," "noble") name that was being defamed and slandered. Believers bear the name of Jesus; it has "been called" over them (cf. Deut. 28:10; Isa. 63:19). The early believers were called "Christians" (Acts 11:26; 26:28; 1 Pet. 4:16). Though perhaps it was given as a reproach, the name *Christian* became a name of honor and beauty.

Two conditional sentences follow: the first is related to fulfilling the law by neighborly love, "You shall love your neighbor as yourself" (v. 8; cf. Lev. 19:18); and the second concerns those who violate the law (v. 9). To fulfill the law means "carrying out, putting into practice" its precepts. It is called the "royal law" because it is the supreme law of human relationships and it is given by the King Himself. Jesus Himself showed how love for God summarized the first tablet of the law, and love for one's neighbor summarized the second (Mark 12:29-31; cf. Rom. 13:8-10; Gal. 5:14). The singular "you" personalizes the command and makes it an individual responsibility. The term *neighbor* in the Levitical context was limited to the community of Israel, but in the parable of the good Samaritan Jesus enlarged it to include anyone in need of help (Luke 10:30-37). He also elevated the standard of love from "love your neighbor as yourself" to "love one another, just as I have loved you" (John 15:12; cf. Matt. 7:12).

The second conditional sentence is in sharp contrast to the first (v. 9). To show partiality is not only not showing love, it is a violation of the law of love; it is a blatant sin. The law demands equality of treatment toward a person, whether he be rich or poor. Partiality is clearly forbidden in the Mosaic law (Lev. 19:15). "Committing" is present tense, stressing the willful, deliberate nature of the act. Those who practice such things are transgressors of the law. *Sin* emphasizes the failure to measure up to the law (Rom. 3:23); being *transgressors* emphasizes the deliberate violation of the divine standard. John wrote, "Sin is lawlessness" (1 John 3:4). Perhaps the people to whom James was writing assumed that they were acting righteously and observing the law in that they welcomed the rich into their assembly; but James points out that their flippant attitude toward the poor was actually a repudiation of the law, for partiality is sin and a transgression of the law they endeavored to keep.

PREJUDICE IS JUDGING WITHOUT PROPER MERCY (2:10-13)

James concludes his argument against prejudice by reminding his readers that any lapse makes one guilty of violating the law (v. 10), for the law must be seen as a unit. To break one law is to be a transgressor (v. 11); therefore a person's whole life, action, and speech must be brought into conformity to the law of liberty (v. 12). A person will be judged in keeping with his mercy or lack or mercy toward others (v. 13).

The principle that to break a part of the law is to make one guilty of the whole is based in the unitary nature of the law (v. 10). The verbs "keep" and "stumble" are in the subjunctive mood, indicating that James is not portraying an actual historical situation, but rather laying down a mental concept. To keep the law is to guard or protect it against any violation. If a person should stumble or trip over the boundary at any one point, he is immediately labeled a transgressor and he becomes guilty.

"Guilty" (*enochos*) means "in the power of." The sinner is brought under the controlling power of the whole law. The verb "has become" is in the perfect tense, denoting a continuing situation or state; he stands guilty. That does not mean that the individual has broken every law, or that some violations are not as serious as others, but it does mean that the one who breaks the law, any part of the law, is before the law condemned.

The unity of the law emanates from the unity of the Lawgiver (v. 11). The same God gave both the seventh commandment, "You shall not commit adultery" (Ex. 20:14), and the sixth one, "You shall not murder" (Ex. 20:13). To violate either is to violate the law of love toward one's neighbor. It is illogical to assume that a person by keeping one of the commandments is free to violate any of the others with impunity. The Lord gave the deeper spiritual meanings of those commandments by teaching that the sin of lust is at the root of adultery, and anger or contempt is at the base of premeditated murder (Matt. 5:21-22, 27-28). A person may not have murdered someone or been unfaithful to his spouse, but to harbor resentment against a brother or sister still makes one a transgressor. Prejudice toward the poor makes one guilty. "You have become," as in verse 10, is in the perfect tense, stressing the permanent reality of being a transgressor. That guilt is individualized and made personal as James moves from the general "whoever" (v. 10) to the more personal and direct "you" (v. 11).

A solemn reminder is given that whether or not one has acted according to the law of liberty, he will be judged by it (v. 12). The two imperatives, "speak" and "act," are present-tense verbs suggesting a habitual way of life. In the illustration, partiality was demonstrated in both speech and action (vv. 2-3); insensitive words had accompanied condescending actions. The importance of right action is developed more fully in 2:14-26, and right speech in chapter 3. The law, called the "perfect law" (1:25) and the "royal law" (2:8) is a "law of liberty" in that it operates not from external coercion but from inner constraint. The word that has been implanted in the heart (1:21) stimulates the believer to a life of active obedience. The awareness of coming judgment motivates the believer inwardly toward holiness in daily life. That the Lord will judge both word and action is a truth found throughout

Scripture. Christ warned His listeners that in the day of judgment they would give an account of every careless word (Matt. 12:36-37). Likewise Paul reminded the Corinthians that they would be judged according to the deeds done in the body (2 Cor. 5:10). He also wrote that God "will render to every man according to his deeds" (Rom. 2:6).

In a climactic manner James categorically insists that the one who has not shown mercy should not expect to receive any himself on the day that it really counts (v. 13). The self-righteous person may fail in his exercise of mercy, or he may even consider the practice of mercy to be a weakness; but God is a merciful God, and He desires mercy from His people (Prov. 21:13). Jesus promised, "Blessed are the merciful, for they shall receive mercy" (Matt. 5:7). Several of the parables teach the two sides of that truth. In the parable of the good Samaritan, the good Samaritan "felt compassion," and he is "the one who showed mercy," though neither the priest nor the Levite exercise any (Luke 10:30-37). In the parable of the sheep and the goats, individuals are judged on the basis of seemingly small acts of compassion and mercy (Matt. 25:32-46). The unmerciful servant in the parable that bears his name is censored and severely punished for his lack of mercy. After having been forgiven much, he is unwilling to forgive his fellow servant. Christ concluded the parable by warning, "So shall My heavenly Father also do to you, if each of you does not forgive his brother from your heart" (Matt. 18:23-35). The principle that what we do to others will be done to us was clearly taught by the Lord: "For if you forgive men for their transgressions, your heavenly Father will also forgive you. But if you do not forgive men, then your Father will not forgive your transgressions" (Matt. 6:14-15).

Though there will be no mercy on judgment day for the one who has shown no mercy, the merciful one will triumph, for mercy will rise victorious over condemnation. That must not be understood to mean that by acts of mercy one can purchase the mercy of God; God's mercy is freely given by His grace. Rather, acts of mercy evidence that the Spirit of God is at work in the heart and the fruit of righteousness is being produced. Obviously mercy does not triumph at the expense of justice. The two must go hand in hand. It was divine mercy that sent Jesus to the cross so that God "might be just and the justifier of the one who has faith in Jesus" (Rom. 3:26). God's mercy was victorious over judgment; in like manner our mercy toward others must triumph over petty acts of prejudice. The psalmist wrote, "I will sing of lovingkindness and justice" (Psalm 101:1).

In verses 12-13 James has primarily final judgment in view. For the believer judgment will be at the judgment seat of Christ, the *Bema* seat (2 Cor. 5:10); for the unbeliever it will be at the great white throne (Rev. 20:11-13). But these verses also set forth a principle of life; the one who expects mercy in this life should be merciful to others (Rom. 15:7).

5

EXHIBITING A PRODUCTIVE FAITH

JAMES 2:14-26

The second section of James 2 continues the consideration of true faith begun in 2:1. As one must not hold the faith in the Lord Jesus and at the same time have personal prejudice toward others (2:1-13), so he should not claim to have faith without having corresponding works. As the law of love demands mercy (v. 13), so genuine faith will produce fruit. James earlier concluded that true religion must have corresponding works or it is worthless (1:26-27); the one who claims true faith must be a doer, not merely a hearer (1:22).

Some have thought that James by emphasizing works is contradicting Paul's emphasis on justification by faith apart from works (Rom. 4); but James is arguing that true faith will produce works. Faith that does not bear fruit is simply not genuine faith. James would agree that works are not the basis of faith, for by the works of the law "no one is justified" (Gal. 3:11). Works are the fruit of true faith; true faith must work through love (Gal. 5:6). Paul writes that though one is saved through faith, and not as a result of works, he is "created in Christ Jesus for good works" (Eph. 2:8-10). Works and faith must go hand in hand.

Evidently the readers, having been saved out of a life of legalism, had tended to go from the one extreme of legalism to the other extreme of license and laxity toward the divine requirements. They felt that being orthodox in doctrine was sufficient, but they were not allowing the Christian faith to affect their whole life-style. They needed to be challenged toward a productive faith.

James argues for a vibrant living faith along three lines. First he shows the deadness of a faith that has no works (2:14-17), then the futility of orthodoxy without works (2:18-20), followed by two Old Testament examples of productive faith (2:21-26).

THE DEADNESS OF A FAITH THAT HAS NO WORKS (2:14-17)

With characteristic abruptness James challenges his readers concerning faith that is only a "wordy" faith. They claimed to hold the faith, yet the lack of mercy shown the impoverished visitor entering their assembly weakened their claim. The abrupt "What use is it" is tempered by the tender "My brethren" (v. 14; cf. 2:1). Christians need to be challenged constantly that verbal assent must be followed by action. By the use of two rhetorical questions, James is not simply telling the readers concerning the uselessness of a nonworking faith, but he is causing them to reason with him and draw a proper conclusion.

The first question introduces a hypothetical situation: an individual claims to have faith, to be a Christian, but has no corresponding works by which to justify that claim. Present tense verbs are used, denoting that this is a way of life; the person repeatedly claims to be a believer, yet there is a continual lack of any external evidence of faith. The question challenges the legitimacy of a profession of faith that produces no corresponding fruit (cf. 1 John 2:4, 6, 9). The context makes it clear that "works" is not to be understood as efforts to attain salvation, but deeds of benevolence such as providing clothing and food (cf. v. 15). Faith has the full soteriological meaning here—faith in the Lord for eternal salvation (cf. v. 1). This hypothetical person is verbally claiming to be saved, but he is bearing no accompanying fruit of righteousness and piety.

The second question, "Can that faith save him?" is presented in such a way as to make the answer self-evident: an emphatic *no*. "Faith" has the article, which refers it back to the previous question. The question is not, "Can faith save?" for indeed it is faith and faith alone that saves; rather the question is, "Can that kind of unproductive, professed faith (mentioned in the first question) save?" "Save" should be understood eschatologically in the sense of final salvation. Ross concludes, "Can the faith that is not accompanied by moral character and conduct save anyone at the judgment seat of God, who is merciless to the man who shows no mercy?"[1] That should not be understood as works-salvation, nor the potential loss of salvation; rather it is a clear affirmation that the one who is genuinely saved will not be unfruitful. Those with authentic faith will persevere in deeds of righteousness.

In the next two verses (vv. 15-16), James draws an illustration of nonworking, noncharitable faith. A similar illustration of the lack of daily needs is used by John (1 John 3:17-18). James, as the leader of the poverty-stricken Jerusalem church (Acts 4:35; 6:1; 11-29-30), was well suited to give this illustration. The hypothetical people of 2:2 were evidently visitors; the one mentioned at this point is portrayed as a member of the assembly. *Brother* and *sister* were terms used by the early church of members of the spiritual family (Rom. 16:1; 1 Cor. 7:15). That James is speaking of a member makes the situation illustrated even more serious, for the church has a primary responsibility toward her own members (Gal. 6:10). The brother or sister is portrayed as both cold and hungry: "without clothing and in need of daily food." The verse need not be understood as implying nakedness (cf. John 21:7); it carries the meaning here of being poorly dressed, being in rags (cf. Matt. 25:36). "In need of daily food" suggests that the individual was without food for even that day.

The heartless response to that theoretical situation is an oral one, coming from one of the members: "Go in peace, be warmed and be filled" (v. 16). "Go in peace" is the customary expression of farewell used by the Jews (cf. Mark 5:34; Luke 7:50). It answers to the Hebrew *shalom* (1 Sam.

1. Alexander Ross, *The Epistles of James and John, The New International Commentary on the New Testament,* ed. F. F. Bruce (Grand Rapids: Eerdmans, 1972), 51.

1:17). The verbs "be warmed" and "be filled," which correspond to the two identified needs, are present passive imperatives meaning essentially, "Let someone else be warming you and feeding you." The failure of Christian charity was not undesigned; it was intentional and persistent. Perhaps it should even be understood as a prayer, "May you be warmed and fed by God," similar to our often flippant "The Lord bless you," or "I am praying for you, brother," or the colloquial "Good luck to you." But even prayer becomes hollow when the law of love is not being fulfilled. The poor beggar, a brother in Christ, has been rejected and is commanded to leave ("go"). He is left undernourished and shivering, still further depressed.

There is an interesting shift here from the singular to the plural. One person was the spokesman for the group, "one of you"; but the group shares in the responsibility for not providing the necessities of life, "You [plural] do not give." Being reproved in the illustration for not providing help suggests that they were physically able to do so, but did not. It was not a case of inability (cf. 1 John 3:17), but rather of unwillingness. In a situation like that, words without accompanying action are without value; therefore the repeated and unanswerable inquiry "What use is that?" (cf. v. 14). Neither the speaker, the group, nor the destitute brother or sister has been benefited.

"Even so" (v. 17) introduces the application wherein James draws an analogy between the illustration (vv. 15-16) and the useless faith of verse 14. A compassion that consists only of words is sheer mockery. That kind of faith is like a body without life. Being dead, it cannot help. If there is true life, it will not remain latent. "By itself" grammatically can go with either "faith" or "dead." It is better to interpret it as qualifying "faith." A faith by itself, which bears no fruit, is for all practical purposes dead in the sense of being unproductive and sterile (cf. Rom. 7:8). Adamson notes the vicious circle: "Faith that produces no works is dead; and dead faith cannot produce works."[2]

---

2. Adamson, 124.

THE FUTILITY OF ORTHODOXY WITHOUT WORKS (2:18-20)

Several technical difficulties are connected with the interpretation of verse 18. Who is the "someone"? Does the quotation end in the middle of the verse, or at the end? And, who are the "you" and the "I"? Some feel that the person speaking is a friendly supporter of James, who is addressing the prevaricator of verse 14. It could be paraphrased something like this: "You allege to have faith; I have works. I can demonstrate my faith by my works, but I challenge you to exhibit your faith without works" (cf. NASB). Adamson paraphrases:

> In effect, James says here: "You claim to have 'faith' and I claim to have 'works,' actions, behavior. I can prove the existence and quality of my 'faith' by my 'works' (actions and behavior), but I defy you to prove (to me or any of the rest of mankind) the existence and/or quality of your 'faith.' For I do not believe that without 'works' (actions and behavior) you can possibly have any genuine 'faith.' "[3]

Another possible solution, though somewhat unnatural, is to view the "someone" as asking the question, "Do you have faith?" or perhaps as making an exclamation, "You claim to have faith!" (Moffatt*). To that inquiry James responds, "I have works; show me your faith. . . ."

Others feel that the one speaking is a fellow believer endeavoring to harmonize the two sides by being tolerant of both positions, suggesting that it is a matter of spiritual gifts: one has the gift of faith, another of works. In that interpretation, the "you" and "I" are understood in the sense of "one says this, and another says that." To that compromiser James challenges, "Show me your faith without the works. . . ." (cf. NEB).

Another, though similar, understanding of this difficult verse is to view the "someone" as an objector to James's position, who seeks to separate faith from works, arguing

---

**A New Translation,* by James Moffatt.

3. Ibid., 125.

that one may have faith without works, or vice versa. He is saying, "You as a Christian have faith, and I as a Jew have works." To that James bursts forth, "Show me your faith without works. . . ." Whatever the exact punctuation may be, the obvious conclusion is that works are necessary as evidence of faith. To prove his point, James draws upon the proposition that "God is one" (v. 19). A variant rendering is, "There is one God" (KJV, NEB). The first rendering emphasizes the unity of the Godhead; the second emphasizes monotheism, there is but one God. The statement "God is one," or "There is one God," is taken from the beginning of the Shema, a portion of Scripture recited morning and evening by an orthodox Jew (Deut. 6:4; cf. Mark 12:29). But intellectual assent to that cardinal point of doctrine, a test of both Christian and Jewish orthodoxy, is not in itself saving faith, for even demons give assent to it.

The sentence may be either a question or a statement. James may be asking, "Do you believe . . ." (Berkeley*), or, as most translations agree, he may be simply stating a position he knows the objector to hold: "You believe . . ." There is common ground on which the objector can be confronted. One does well to have an orthodox faith, but intellectual affirmation alone is woefully deficient. Even the very archenemies of God, the demons, are knowledgeable and fully accepting of the uniqueness and unity of God. Demons are not skeptics, agnostics, or atheists. But the orthodox man with inoperative faith is no better than they. Demons mentioned in the gospels frequently acknowledged the existence and power of God, but that did not change their diabolical character and behavior (Matt. 8:29; Mark 5:7; Luke 4:41; cf. Acts 19:15; 1 Tim. 4:1).

James points out that at least the demons, in light of their knowledge, fear, even shudder. The verb "shudder" means "bristle." It portrays hair standing on end. Demons are aware that in the end the forces of God will triumph over the

---

**Berkeley Version in Modern English.*

forces of evil (Matt. 8:29; 25:41). The frightful prospect of their end makes them shudder in terror. In a subtle manner, the orthodox man with an inoperative faith is reminded of the terror of the Lord upon those who have not believed with a character-changing faith.

The conclusion to the argument about dead orthodoxy is that a faith that has no corresponding works is barren and unproductive (v. 20). The "but" introduces a transitional sentence between the argument just stated and the two Scriptural examples of a working faith in the next verses. "Are you willing to recognize" suggests that the objector is unwilling to face squarely the issue as it has been presented, and therefore James will give historical proof from the lives of two Old Testament characters. The objector is labeled "foolish" (*kene*), meaning "empty, defective." There is a hollowness about this person; he is devoid of a living faith, and what faith he has is a sham. Both "faith" and "works" have the definite article ("the faith without the works"), pointing back to the type of faith and works under discussion. The kind of faith that has no works is "useless" (*argē*), meaning "not working," hence "idle, unproductive," or "barren." There is an interesting and subtle play on words between "works" (*ergōn*) and "useless" (*argē*), a faith without works is unworking. A verbal commitment to orthodoxy without resulting fruit is unproductive.

EXAMPLES OF PRODUCTIVE FAITH (2:21-26)

Having reasoned that faith must have fruit or it is both dead (v. 17) and unproductive (v. 20), James uses two illustrations from the Old Testament to demonstrate the presence and reality of living, operative faith. The first example is that of Abraham (vv. 21-24), and the second of Rahab (v. 25). In verse 26 he makes his concluding statement that "faith without works is dead."

Using Abraham, the father of the nation of Israel, as an example of living faith would surely catch the attention of the Jewish readers. Both Paul and the writer to the Hebrews also use Abraham as an outstanding example of faith (Rom. 4;

Gal. 3:6-9; Heb. 11:8-19). "Our father" (v. 21) suggests that James was primarily writing to Jews, though Abraham is also the spiritual father of all who believe (Gal. 3:7, 29).

James is endeavoring to make the point that the great patriarch Abraham had a working faith by which he was justified. "Justified" can be understood in two different ways. It may mean "to be vindicated, to be shown to be right." In that sense Abraham's ready obedience to God's command to sacrifice his son vindicated or justified the declaration that he had been made righteous (cf. Rom. 3:4; 1 Tim. 3:16). His action demonstrated that he had been justified. Or the term may mean "to acquit, to pronounce righteous." Abraham's faith, mentioned in Genesis 15:6, was a working faith as evidenced by his willingness to offer his son (Gen. 22). It was that faith, the faith that characterized his life, that resulted in justification. James is not arguing for justification by works apart from faith, but rather for faith at work.

The offering up of Isaac took place thirty or forty years after Abraham was accounted righteous. The declaration of his righteousness came when he took God at His word and believed that he would become the father of a multitude of people. The writer to the Hebrews gives the situation mentioned by James: "He [Abraham] who had received the promises was offering up his only begotten son" (11:17). "Offered up" is in the aorist tense, indicating that though the action was halted before it was completed (Gen. 22:10-13), Abraham had fully intended to go through with the sacrifice of his son. God expressed His approval of Abraham's obedience when He said, "Do not stretch out your hand against the lad, and do nothing to him; for now I know that you fear God, since you have not withheld your son, your only son, from Me" (Gen. 22:12).

The logical and convincing deduction from verse 21 is that faith and works are inseparable (v. 22). Though verse 22 may be rendered as a question, it fits better as a statement of fact. Both the "you see" (*blepeis*) here and the "you see" (*horate*) in verse 24 tie in as responses to the question "Are you willing to recognize?" (v. 20). "You see" (v. 22), being singular, is addressed to the objector of verses 14, 18, and 19. "Faith" has the article, which refers to the faith of Abraham, something that, though not mentioned in verse 21, is clearly assumed. His works were a product of his faith. The verb "was working with" is in the imperfect tense, underscoring the continuous working cooperation between faith and works. Paul speaks of "faith working through love" (Gal. 5:6).

James lists three results of that working faith. First, it was by works that Abraham's faith was perfected. Both "works" and "faith" have the article, pointing specifically to the works and faith of Abraham: "As a result of the [his] works, the [his] faith was perfected." That Abraham's faith was perfected by his works implied that his faith came first, and that it was matured by his works. "Was perfected" means "to be brought to its intended goal." "A fruit tree is made perfect, brought to its intended goal, by the fruit which it produces."[4] The believer is saved by faith for good works. The verb, being in the passive voice, suggests that it is God who brings about the perfecting.

Second, not only was Abraham's faith perfected, but also Scripture was fulfilled (v. 23; cf. Gen. 15:6). The offering of Isaac occurred many years after Abraham was accounted righteous, but his willing surrender of the child of promise, with the knowledge that God was able to raise him from the dead, proved the reality of Abraham's faith. In that sense Genesis 15:6 is somewhat prophetic of the events of Genesis 22. Paul used that same quotation to prove justification by faith apart from works (Rom. 4:3; Gal. 3:6), but Paul's point was that a person is saved apart from human effort in the earning of salvation. He demonstrated that Abraham was saved before the rite of circumcision (Rom. 4:10; cf. Gen. 17:9-27) and before the coming of the Mosaic law (Rom.

---

4. Hiebert, 194.

4:13). Thus Paul argues that neither religious rite nor legalism will bring justification. James introduces neither the merits of circumcision nor those of law. His point is that saving faith will lead to godly obedience. Abraham's obedience demonstrated the reality of his faith. The Christian is saved by faith alone, but not by a faith that is alone. God accounted Abraham's act of faith to be the right action that would spring from a heart of one who years before had been declared righteous by faith.

The third result of Abraham's working faith was that "he was called a friend of God." Though James does not directly quote any Old Testament passage, both 2 Chronicles 20:7 and Isaiah 41:8 speak of Abraham as being a friend of God. Perhaps James had in mind the events of Genesis 18:17-19. God did not hide from Abraham His plans but treated him as a friend by revealing to him His purposes. It was that type of intimate relationship that the apostle John laid claim to when he identified himself as the disciple "whom Jesus loved" (John 13:23; cf. 13:1). Jesus claimed His disciples as His friends (John 15:14). The child of God, living in obedience to His will, is like faithful Abraham, a friend of God.

Having addressed and effectively refuted the objector, James now turns to all his readers with the plural "You see" (v. 24), to give the formal, undeniable answer to the question of verse 14. In stating his conclusion, James insists on the inseparableness of faith and works. He does not conclude that man is justified by works and not by faith, but that he is justified by works and not faith alone. James believes in justification by faith, but not a faith that has no works. The example of Abraham demonstrated that there is the initial act of faith, followed by the expression of faith in active obedience. The sanctified life grows out of the initial step of faith.

The second example of operative faith is Rahab (v. 25; cf. Josh. 2:1-21). There is a striking contrast between these two examples. She was a pagan, immoral, Canaanite woman, in contrast to Abraham, the father of the faithful. No doubt

James uses Rahab to show that a person from the most degrading background is not out of the reach of God's grace. Salvation includes both patriarch and prostitute. Jewish tradition shows a considerable interest in Rahab. She was regarded as a forerunner of the proselytes and was said to have become the wife of Joshua and the mother of many prophets. Matthew included her name in the genealogy of the Lord (Matt. 1:5).

Though the book of Hebrews lists her as a woman of faith (11:31), James makes no mention of her faith. He simply assumes that his readers are aware of it. The evidence of faith is twofold. First, she "received" the messengers. The verb suggests a friendly reception. Then she assured their safety by sending "them out by another way." According to Joshua 2:11, she acknowledged that God "is God in heaven above and on earth beneath" and acted out her faith in a daring manner, without concern for personal safety. It is interesting that Clement of Rome in his first epistle to the Corinthians (c. A.D. 95-100) refers to both Abraham and Rahab as examples of "faith and hospitality" (1 Clem. 10, 12). Those two very diverse examples of working faith demonstrate the wide range of activities that can spring from an operative faith.

In the concluding statement of James's argument, faith is compared to the human body and works to its spirit (v. 26). At first glance it might seem more appropriate to reverse the comparison and speak of the body as works and the spirit as faith. But that is precisely the point. To James a sterile faith is like a corpse—works evidence life. "Spirit" (*pneumatos*) may be understood as "breath." As breathing is a sign of life, so works are a sign of genuine faith. More likely though, it speaks of the vital principle of life. A body without life is dead; so also faith without the vital principle of works is dead. With that blunt conclusion, James lets his case rest.

6

CONTROLLING THE TONGUE

JAMES 3:1-12

Christian works, concerning which James has just written (2:14-26), also include the use of the tongue. A true mark of Christian maturity is the proper control of one's speech. The subject of the tongue was introduced earlier, at which time the readers were counseled to be "slow to speak" (1:19) and to bridle the tongue (1:26). The bridled tongue introduces the imagery of 3:2-3. This section concerning the tongue can be divided into four parts: the importance of a controlled tongue (vv. 1-2), the need for the control of the tongue (vv. 3-6), the difficulty in controlling the tongue (vv. 7-8), and the inconsistency of an uncontrolled tongue (vv. 9-12).

THE IMPORTANCE OF A CONTROLLED TONGUE (3:1-2)

In 1:19, when speaking concerning the control of the tongue, James is addressing the whole body. At this point he addresses those who are and those who desire to be teachers. Because the early church was patterned somewhat after the synagogue, the teachers in the church had a position of dignity and responsibility similar to that of the rabbis in the synagogue. Perhaps some aspiring to the position were unqualified or did not realize the responsibilities inherent in the job. They needed to be warned about the power inherent in the tongue.

That the church must have teachers is self-evident (Acts 2:42). From the divine standpoint, the Spirit sovereignly endows certain ones with the gift of teaching (1 Cor. 12:28) and those with the gift of teaching are given to the Body (Eph. 4:11). From the human perspective, as the church looks for leadership she is commanded to select elders who, among other things, are "able to teach" (1 Tim. 3:2). Spiritual men in the body may aspire to become elders and assume teaching responsibilities (1 Tim. 3:1); but those seeking to be teachers in the body must search their motives, recognize the great responsibility, and determine to control that member of their body, the tongue, which is so heavily utilized in the exercise of their gift.

The use of "my brethren" (v. 1) indicates that James is writing to believers, not false teachers. By using "we" he includes himself among the teachers and acknowledges that as a member of that privileged group he too will be under the "stricter judgment." There are various rewards that come from teaching, such as status, honor, and a following, but with them goes grave responsibility. Jesus said, "From everyone who has been given much shall much be required" (Luke 12:48). Paul warned Timothy about being too hasty in ordaining anyone to church leadership because of the grave responsibilities which went with it (1 Tim. 5:22). Judgment at the judgment seat of Christ (2 Cor. 5:10) will be on the principle that the greater the influence, the greater the responsibility. If every person will give account on the day of judgment for every careless word spoken (Matt. 12:36), how much more the teacher, whose implement of trade is the tongue (cf. Heb. 13:17)! That was not meant to discourage the true teacher who is gifted of God for the ministry of teaching, but rather to challenge him concerning the seriousness of the task. It is also a warning to those who aspire to be teachers but have not been called of God for the task. They place themselves in great jeopardy.

The problem of the tongue addressed in the following verses applies in a special way to teachers, but it is also a problem that all believers face; therefore James moves from the teacher to Christians in general. There is nothing in verses 2-12 that does not apply to all members of the church as well as to the teachers. All believers stumble; all have difficulty controlling the tongue.

The universality of sin is clear: "We all stumble" (v. 2). The verb "stumble," used also in 2:10, indicates a mistake that is blameworthy, a moral lapse. The use of the present tense denotes repeated action; it occurs again and again. Scripture asserts, "All have sinned" (Rom. 3:23), and, "If we say that we have no sin, we are deceiving ourselves" (1 John 1:8; cf. 1 Kings 8:46; Prov. 20:9; Rom. 3:9). Not only do all repeatedly stumble, but all do so "in many ways." The sin of the tongue is one among many, though a very significant one. When Paul lists five different organs of the body that are vehicles of sin—throat, tongue, lips, mouth, and feet (Rom. 3:13-15)—it is informative that four of the five relate to speech.

So important is the tongue that if a person can control it, "he is a perfect man," for he has his whole body under control. He has come to spiritual maturity (cf. the use of "perfect" in 1:4). Earlier James wrote of bridling the tongue (1:26); now he speaks of bridling the whole body. If the most trying and difficult member of the body can be controlled, it follows that the whole body can be controlled. The horse is bridled to control its body and to direct its steps; so the body is to be brought under control and used as an instrument of righteousness. James is not arguing for silence, but for the wise, effective use of the tongue. Our Lord Jesus is the supreme example of the controlled use of the tongue (1 Pet. 2:21-23).

THE NEED FOR THE CONTROL OF THE TONGUE (3:3-6)

Little things can have far-reaching effects, and though the tongue is little, it has great potential for both usefulness and destruction. Three illustrations are utilized to demonstrate the point: the horse's bit (v. 3), a ship's rudder (v. 4), and fire (vv. 5-6). The first two portray the usefulness of a small item in controlling something many times its size; the third graphically illustrates the potentially destructive power of something that at its beginning may be very insignificant.

The introduction of bridle (v. 2) leads easily to the illustration of bridle and bit (v. 3). The noun translated "bit" comes from the verb earlier translated "bridle." Here the reference is to that part of the bridle put into the horse's mouth, the bit. The purpose for the bridle and bit is "so that they [horses] may obey us." Control of the horse's mouth results in control of his body. The two uses of "we" indicate that James was using a figure familiar to his readers, a common experience of daily life. They knew by common experience how a small bit could be used to harness the power of a strong animal.

The second illustration is the ship's rudder (v. 4). A small rudder, an oar or paddle-like projection from the ship's stern, is able to direct a large ship, even in the face of adverse winds. As slight pressure on the bit will direct a horse, so movement of the rudder adjusts the direction of the ship. James emphasizes the magnitude of the vessel and the force of contrary winds in contrast to the smallness of the rudder. That figure would also be familiar to his readers. The ship in which Paul was shipwrecked had 276 people aboard and a cargo of wheat (Acts 27:37-38). Apparently it was equipped with two rudders (Acts 27:40).

"Inclination" (*hormē,* "motion, impulse") may refer either to the physical pressure applied to the tiller by the pilot, or to the pilot's personal desire or inclination. Translations vary: "Wherever the pilot wants to go" (NIV), "Wherever the will of the pilot directs" (RSV), "Whithersoever the force of the governor wills" (DV*). Mayor translates it in whichever direction "the pressure (touch) of the steersman decides."[1] "The pilot" (*tou euthunontos,* "the one who makes level, who leads straight") is the one who is actually handling the tiller. He has at his command, by controlling the rudder, the course of the whole ship.

Though the two analogies (the bit and the rudder) have in

**Douay Version.*

1. Mayor, 111.

mind primarily the contrast between the small implements and the large bodies they control, a contrast between the two figures is also significant. The bit controls an animate body, a power from within; whereas the rudder controls an inanimate body by using to its advantage both the favorable and unfavorable external powers of wind and current.

The point of the two illustrations is to emphasize that the tongue, though small, "boasts of great things" (v. 5). That phrase can be understood in one of two ways. It may mean that the tongue is haughty, with a false sense of importance, as in Psalm 12:3, "The tongue that speaks great things." But it more probably means that the tongue has great power; through the use of the tongue great things can be accomplished and incalculable power released. The latter meaning fits the context better.

That great power, which should be harnessed for good, can also do much damage. The imagery now changes to the devastating results of a forest fire: "Behold, how great a forest is set aflame by such a small fire!" "Forest" refers to wood, either standing timber or cut lumber. Translations vary from "huge stack of timber" (NEB) to "a great forest" (NIV; cf. RSV). Douay uses the older English, "a great wood." "Set aflame," meaning "light up," hence "kindle," emphasizes the starting of a fire. The tongue, through malicious gossip or careless speech, can spark conflagrations ruinous to the well-being of the church. Proverbs 16:27 reads: "A worthless man digs up evil, while his words are as a scorching fire."

Having given the illustration of fire, James proceeds to explain the metaphor, "The tongue is a fire" (v. 6). Like fire, the tongue is potentially dangerous and destructive if left uncontrolled. The punctuation of what follows is difficult. "The very world of iniquity" may be set in opposition to what precedes: "The tongue is a fire, the very world of iniquity" (NASB), or it may be related to what follows as a predicate nominative: "The tongue is an unrighteous world among our members" (RSV). The NIV seeks to combine the two possibilities: "The tongue also is a fire, a world of evil among the parts of the body." However one may seek to punctuate the verse, it is evident that the caustic style employed by James evidences intense indignation against the evils of the tongue.

Several things are said about the tongue. First, it is the "very world of iniquity." "World" (*kosmos*) originally meant "orderliness," or "adornment" (cf. 1 Pet. 3:3). If that is the connotation James had in mind, the meaning would be that the tongue is an adornment for evil; it makes evil to appear good. The term, however, came to mean an *orderly system*. If that is the meaning, then the tongue is said to be a vast system of iniquity, an entire moral system that is opposed and alien to God. That is the more typical use of the term (cf. 1:27; 4:4; John 12:31). A less likely meaning of "world" is "sum total of" as in the KJV, "a world of iniquity."

Second, the tongue "is set among our members." The verb "is set" ("is appointed, is constituted") can be either middle or passive; either "sets itself" or "is set." It is the same form as found in 4:4, "makes himself." In light of the context, the middle is preferred. The tongue established itself to rule over the members of the body by self-appointment. The member that should be used as an instrument of grace to the hearer (Luke 4:22; Col. 4:6) becomes as uncontrolled fire, a vast system of evil.

Third, the member "defiles the entire body." By permitting itself to be an instrument for so much sin, it effectively defiles the whole person. Paul speaks of the "unwholesome word" (Eph. 4:29; lit., "rotten"). He also mentions "filthiness and silly talk, or coarse jesting" (Eph. 5:4). Those should not be a part of the Christian's vocabulary. Though He used a different term for "defile," Jesus reminded His listeners, "Not what enters into the mouth defiles the man, but what proceeds out of the mouth, this defiles the man" (Matt. 15:11). In 1:27, the world is said to be that which stains the person. Pollution can come from both without (world) and within (tongue). "The entire body" is not limited to the physical, as in verse 3; the entire personality can be defiled.

Fourth, the tongue "sets on fire the course of our life." Because the two terms translated "course" and "life" are both capable of several meanings, translations vary widely. Some examples are: "the course of nature" (KJV), "the wheel of nature" (ASV), "the wheel of our existence" (NEB), "the cycle of nature" (RSV), "the whole machinery of existence" (Berkeley). It may carry the idea of our whole life cycle, from birth to death, being set aflame by the tongue. Or similarly, it may speak of the cycles and routines of everyday life being set ablaze by the vicious, uncontrolled tongue. Perhaps it is better to understand it as the whole area of human existence in all its social relationships being affected by conflagrations from the untamed tongue.

Finally, the tongue "is set on fire by hell." The tongue can be set on fire by the gracious Spirit of God to produce the peaceful fruit of righteousness, or it can be set on fire from the pit of hell. Hell (lit., "Gehenna") is the place of punishment for the unbelieving dead (Matt. 10:28). Outside of the gospels this is the only place where the term is used in the New Testament. *Gehenna* is the Greek name for the Valley of Hinnom, a valley immediately south of Jerusalem that was used as the dumping ground for the city's refuse. The continually burning rubbish heap became a fitting picture of the eternal sufferings of those in the place of judgment. Jesus spoke of the "hell [*Gehenna*] of fire" (Matt. 5:22) as the place "where their worm does not die, and the fire is not quenched" (Mark 9:48; cf. Isa. 66:24). The term *Gehenna* also seems to be used as the seat of Satan's operations. Jesus spoke of a proselyte to Pharisaism as becoming a "son of hell [*Gehenna*]" (Matt. 23:15). That would be similar to saying, "son of Satan" (cf. John 8:44). The uncontrolled tongue can be inflamed by Satan himself. It is of interest that James has united three subversive tenets: the world, the flesh, and Satan. The tongue is a key instrument through which those three can vent their evil.

THE DIFFICULTY IN CONTROLLING THE TONGUE (3:7-8)

Having set forth the diabolical nature of the tongue, James

proceeds to show how difficult it is to bring it under control. Man can dominate the animal world (v. 7), but the mischievous tongue remains outside his control (v. 8). The backdrop to verse 7 is the creation account. Man was to "rule over the fish of the sea and over the birds of the sky and over the cattle and over all the earth, and over every creeping thing that creeps on the earth" (Gen. 1:26; cf. v. 28). James in customary biblical style divides the creation kingdom into four groups: those that walk, fly, crawl, and swim (cf. Psalm 8:7-8; 1 Cor. 15:39). The term translated "tame" does not mean "domesticate," but rather "subdue, subjugate," or "restrain." The word is used in the account of the demoniac: "No one was strong enough to subdue [tame] him" (Mark 5:4). Both the present and perfect tenses are used, indicating that both now and in the past creatures are being and have been brought under the control of man (Gen. 9:2; Psalm 8:6-8). To have dominion is still man's God-given mandate.

The sad fact is that the one who has been called to rule is unable to tame his own tongue (v. 8). Only by the power of God is anyone enabled to control his tongue; such a person is called "a perfect man" (v. 2). Two pictures are given of the uncontrolled tongue: a restless evil and deadly poison. "Restless" is the adjective used in 1:8, translated "unstable." It portrays an untamed animal restlessly pacing back and forth in its cage ready to pounce on anyone who dares come near. The tongue is also "full of deadly poison." In speaking of depraved man, Paul quoted from the psalmist, "The poison of asps is under their lips" (Rom. 3:13; cf. Pss. 38:4; 140:3). Hurtful gossip and whispered slander can be destructive to innocent people and devastating to the body. Satan, the serpent of old, was called by Christ a murderer, a liar, and the father of lies (John 8:44; cf. 1 John 3:8). It was through the tongue that Satan tempted Eve, and Eve enticed Adam. In setting forth the deeper meanings of the Decalogue, Jesus equated murder with being angry with or saying, "Raca" (lit., "empty-head"), or, "You fool," to a brother (Matt. 5:21-22). A person's reputation and self-esteem can be destroyed through the malicious tongue. As Solomon said,

"Death and life are in the power of the tongue" (Prov. 18:21).

THE INCONSISTENCY OF AN UNCONTROLLED TONGUE (3:9-11)

The most sublime function of the human tongue is to bless God, yet this same instrument curses man (v. 9). To curse man is preposterous and contrary to reason, for man whom we curse bears the image of God, whom we bless. In the Jewish community, every time the name of God was mentioned the phrase "Blessed be He" was added. Evidently the Christian church had also adopted that formula (Eph. 1:3; 1 Pet. 1:3). "Bless" means "speak well of, extol," or "praise." To bless God as Lord and Father is a noble Christian exercise. The terms *Lord* and *Father* emphasize two characteristics, respectively. God is both Lord, emphasizing sovereignty, and Father, suggesting His compassion and love (1:27; Matt. 11:25). As a son bears the image of his father, so mankind bears the image of God the Father. Malachi quizzes, "Do we not all have one father? Has not one God created us?" (Mal. 2:10).

That man is in the image of God suggests an ability to know and serve God; to have will, self-consciousness, and reason, to be a personal, rational, and moral being. It is that divine stamp upon our soul that relates us to God. Because man is in the image of God, he is God's appointed representative over His creation (Gen. 1:26-28; Ps. 8:4-8).

To curse man is to curse God's image, just as to murder man is to strike out against His image (Gen. 9:6). No matter how one might define total depravity, it is evident that, though in the Fall the image of God was greatly impaired, it was not annihilated. The verb "have been made" is in the perfect tense, implying that the image of God has not been completely effaced; every individual reflects to some extent the likeness of God. To curse any person is to be disrespectful to God. James does not separate himself from the rebuke but uses the personal "we."

To utter forth blessing and cursing from the same source is

incongruous (v. 10). Though there is a legitimate use of the curse (Gen. 9:25; Deut. 27:15-26; Josh. 6:26), James is speaking of the uncontrolled verbal abuse that can come about during embittered controversies. As stated earlier, "The anger of man does not achieve the righteousness of God" (1:20). The term *ought* occurs only here in the New Testament. It indicates something completely out of character; something utterly incongruous, which ought not to happen, was happening. To bless God and at the same time curse members of God's family is abnormal and out of harmony with wholesome family relationships. The sum total of the law is to love unequivocally both God and neighbor, not to bless the one and curse the other.

James again uses analogies from nature to prove his point. The first illustration is that of a spring of water (v. 11). A thirsty traveler would not normally expect a spring of water to gush forth alternately "fresh and bitter water." "Bitter" refers to brackish, distasteful, nauseating water. The original readers living near Palestine would be familiar from their own experience with that imagery. They were familiar with springs and wells that produced good water, and others that produced bad water. But the water that would pour forth from a given source would not change from one kind of water to another; it remained constant. The tongue, though, is so fickle that at one time words of grace are spoken, then often in the next moment violent outbursts of anger spew forth.

The second illustration is taken from agriculture, using three of the most common horticultural products of Palestine: the fig, the olive, and the grape vine (v. 12). Each of those remains true to itself; it will not produce what it is not. Christ explained, "You will know them by their fruits. Grapes are not gathered from thorn bushes, nor figs from thistles, are they?" (Matt. 7:16). In nature trees and vines produce what they are meant to produce; each produces after "their kind" (Gen. 1:11). The human tongue, though, is inconsistent. It was made to bless God, but all too often it utters curses against the very creation of God. What should be the servant of God becomes an accomplice of the enemy of God.

The concluding analogy is the inconceivableness of a salty spring producing fresh water. A freshwater lake will have fresh water, and a saltwater lake will have salt water. One does not go to the Dead Sea (the Salt Sea) to draw fresh water. But the human tongue, contrary to nature, is inconsistent and fickle. The uncontrollable tongue is in desperate need of the controlling influence of the Spirit of God.

7

DEMONSTRATING GODLY WISDOM

JAMES 3:13-18

After the digression into the power and misuse of the tongue (3:2-12), James returns to his admonition to Christian teachers, which began in 3:1. Though the material relates primarily to teachers in the Christian church, there is nothing in it that cannot also be applied to every believer. Just as all Christians are responsible to bring the tongue under control, so also all Christians need to demonstrate godly wisdom. This section can be divided into three parts: the appeal to demonstrate true wisdom (v. 13), the demonstration of earth-bound wisdom (vv. 14-16), and the demonstration of the higher wisdom (vv. 17-18).

THE APPEAL TO DEMONSTRATE TRUE WISDOM (3:13)

As in 2:14, 4:1, and 5:13, James uses a rhetorical question to introduce the new topic: "Who among you is wise and understanding?" Using the question forces the readers to think and make a mental response. James, being a leading spokesman in the early church, no doubt used that method effectively in his public preaching. Jesus Himself was skilled in the use of the question (Mark 4:21, 30). That James is addressing teachers primarily is clear from the use of "wise and understanding." "Wise" (*sophos*) is no doubt used here as a technical term for teaching (cf. 3:1). To the Greek, a wise man was one who had achieved a high degree of abstract knowledge; but to the Jew, wisdom was more than academic knowledge in solving theoretical problems. The wise person was one who had practical moral insight based on a knowledge of God and His will. He was one who could give godly advice on practical issues of conduct. Solomon asserted, "The fear of the Lord is the beginning of wisdom" (Prov. 9:10). "Understanding" implies being a specialist, an expert. It carries the idea of having professional knowledge of a field. Those two terms, "wise" and "understanding," are used synonymously in Deuteronomy 1:13, 15; 4:6 (LXX), and probably here as well.

Having warned previously about the ever-present dangers latent in the tongue, James now warns the would-be teachers, who see themselves as wise and experts in their subject matter, that life-style is as important as intellectual acumen. Achievement of abstract knowledge must not be disassociated from moral and spiritual insight and manner of life. Just as genuine faith must be operative and result in works (2:18), so true wisdom must lead to a good and godly life-style. The results will show in both cases: true faith will show itself by works, and true wisdom will also show itself by deeds. The noun "deeds" is the same word as that translated "works" in 2:18. "Behavior" refers to one's daily conduct or life-style (1 Tim. 4:12; 1 Pet. 1:15; 2:12).

The Christian life-style is to be "good," in the sense of beautiful and attractive. Peter writes of "chaste and respectful" (1 Pet. 3:2), "good" (1 Pet. 3:16), and "holy" (2 Pet. 3:11) behavior. The attractiveness of that kind of life will be shown by deeds that spring from "gentleness of wisdom." The primary characteristic of good behavior is "gentleness." The godly teacher will not be arrogant, boastful, or contemptuous; rather he will conduct himself in the gentleness of true wisdom. Using the same term, Jesus, the master teacher, spoke of Himself as being "gentle and humble in heart" (Matt. 11:29). Paul wrote of the "meekness and gentleness of Christ" (2 Cor. 10:1). Perhaps there were self-assertive teachers in the Christian community to which James was writing who needed to be chided concerning their attitude. A wisdom-controlled life will not be characterized by obtrusiveness. Though the Greeks and the world in general equated gentleness with weakness, it is a sign of strength in the Body of Christ (Matt. 20:25-28).

THE DEMONSTRATION OF EARTHBOUND WISDOM (3:14-16)

The "but" (*de*) introduces the dire consequences when godly wisdom is not present. From this point on two types of wisdom are discussed: wisdom limited to this world, earthbound wisdom that does not take into account the divine dimension; and the wisdom from above, from God. Paul makes a similar contrast between the two wisdoms in 1 Corinthians 1-2. He speaks of the "wisdom of the wise" (1:19), and "wisdom of the world" (1:20), the "world through its wisdom" (1:21), "wise according to the flesh" (1:26), and the "wisdom of men" (2:5). That earthly wisdom is contrasted with the "wisdom of God" (1:21, 24, 30; 2:7). The wisdom of God can only be understood by the believer because he has the Spirit (1 Cor. 2:12-15), but the individual without the Spirit does not and cannot possess divine wisdom (1 Cor. 2:14). Paul's emphasis is on the capacity to understand God's wisdom; James's emphasis is on the behavior and life-style that result from the wisdom from above.

An individual, by observing his behavior, may determine the source of his wisdom. "Bitter jealousy and selfish ambition" are two evidences of earthly wisdom. "Jealousy" (*zēlon,* zeal) may be used in a good sense (2 Cor. 11:2), but it usually carries a bad connotation. Here it has the adjective "bitter," which may be understood as "harsh" or "contentious." Teachers may tend toward rivalry; and there is the resulting potential for hard feelings due to advancement or achievement, real or imagined. The second evil is "selfish ambition," which speaks of promoting one's own views or concerns for personal advantage; it is the promoting of self at the expense of others in the Body. Paul lists those two evils among the works of the flesh (Gal. 5:20; cf. 2 Cor. 12:20). Because the heart is the source of attitudes and actions (Matt. 15:19), James speaks of those two hurtful things as being "in your heart."

Teachers who are bitterly jealous and concerned only with

personal advancement are given a double command: "Do not be arrogant and so lie against the truth." The negative "not" (*mē*) goes with both present imperatives, demanding both actions to cease: "Stop being arrogant and stop lying." To be arrogant suggests someone gloating over another person, being superior to another. That also is a common vice found among those teachers whose lives are not characterized by "gentleness of wisdom." Such a person is said to "lie against the truth." He is repudiating the truth. Paul also speaks of "those who are selfishly ambitious and do not obey the truth" (Rom. 2:8). "Truth" may refer to the facts in a case, the truth; or it may speak of the truth of the gospel. If the second meaning is the case, the so-called wise teachers were actually living a lie against the gospel. Life-style may deny and repudiate what the tongue is teaching. One cannot teach effectively the love, mercy, and gentleness of Christ while being jealous and self-seeking. It would be living a lie against the gospel.

James proceeds to characterize earthbound wisdom (v. 15). "This wisdom" refers back to the professed wisdom of verse 14, wisdom that lacks gentleness. It is not the wisdom "which comes down from above." "From above" is a Jewish way of saying "from God" (John 3:3, 7). God the Father gives good things to His children (1:17); surely He cannot be the source of that counterfeit wisdom.

Professed wisdom that results in jealousy and self-seeking is characterized by three adjectives: "earthly, natural, demonic." It is earthly in that its horizons do not go beyond this earth. It is limited to the frail and finite existence of man. Such wisdom originates from man's earthbound ingenuity apart from God. Paul calls it the "wisdom of the world" (1 Cor. 1:20) as opposed to the "wisdom of God" (1 Cor. 1:24). That wisdom is also "natural" (*psuchikē*). It relates to the natural rather than the spiritual. The term, the adjectival form of the word translated "soul" or "life" (*psuchē*), describes that which is essentially human, man as he is in Adam (1 Cor. 15:45). It is that which characterizes the nonspiritual man, the one who is not yet awakened by the Spirit of God. Paul clarifies: "A natural man does not accept the things of the Spirit of God; for they are foolishness to him, and he cannot understand them, because they are spiritually appraised" (1 Cor. 2:14; cf. Jude 19). The third adjective is "demonic." The word comes from the common term *demon.* That wisdom is a wisdom characteristic of or proceeding from an evil spirit. Instead of being influenced by the Spirit of God, it originates out of the demonic world. False teachings are the "doctrines of demons" (1 Tim. 4:1; cf. 1 John 4:1). Hostility in the body is not merely personality conflict; James traces it back to its true source, the hosts of darkness.

Where "jealousy and selfish ambition" exist, one can see the flesh at work (v. 16). The consequences of that which was introduced in verse 14 are "disorder and every evil thing." The adjectival form of the noun *disorder* occurs in 1:8 ("unstable") and in 3:8 ("restless"). Earthly wisdom has the effect of throwing people into confusion, rivalry, antagonism, and anarchy; whereas the wisdom of God brings about goodwill, furthers fellowship, and unites the body. In the disharmony created by jealousy and rivalry is found "every evil thing." The adjective "evil" speaks of that which is the opposite of good, that which is vile and good-for-nothing. Earthly wisdom is without moral value. Because it is without good, it cannot come as a gift of the One who gives only good gifts (1:17; Matt. 7:11).

THE DEMONSTRATION OF THE HIGHER WISDOM (3:17-18)

In contrast to the earthbound wisdom is the wisdom "from above." Earlier James used a present participle with "from above": "comes down from above" (v. 15), indicating that God's wisdom is continually descending, there is a constant supply (cf. 1:17). That true wisdom comes from God is a truth communicated throughout Scripture. Solomon wrote, "The Lord gives wisdom" (Prov. 2:6; cf. Prov. 8:22-31). He himself received his wisdom as a gift of God (2 Chron.

1:7-12). James mentioned previously that those who lack wisdom should "ask of God" (1:5). The wisdom of God is revealed "through the Spirit; for the Spirit searches all things, even the depths of God" (1 Cor. 2:10).

Eight characteristics of God-given wisdom are enumerated by James. This list bears similarity to other lists in the New Testament that speak of the Christian way of life: the description of true love (1 Cor. 13:4-7), the fruit of the Spirit (Gal. 5:22-23), the godly mind-set (Phil. 4:8), and the life-style of the new man (Col. 3:12-15). Our Lord, "who became to us wisdom from God" (1 Cor. 1:30), exemplified perfectly these characteristics. As the believer grows in Christlikeness, these traits become increasingly visible in his life; he is "being transformed into the same [Christ's] image from glory to glory" (2 Cor. 3:18; cf. Col. 3:10; 1 John 3:2-3).

The first characteristic is "pure," an inner quality. Godly wisdom is clean and uncontaminated by such evils as jealousy and selfish ambition. Though not using the same Greek term, Paul wrote, "The goal of our instruction is love from a pure heart and a good conscience and a sincere faith" (1 Tim. 1:5). The teacher who possesses godly wisdom is free from ulterior motives. He seeks to be like Christ, his pattern, free from any kind of moral contamination (1 John 3:3). That trait is identified as "first" because it is foundational to all those that follow.

Purity is followed by seven external characteristics, the first of which is "peaceable." That is a key term in the list because of the dissension being addressed in the context of chapters 3 and 4. Worldly wisdom makes for strife, but heavenly wisdom is peace making—it promotes peace. It is also "gentle." Though there is no exact equivalent to this word in the English language, it speaks of one who is fair, considerate, reasonable, and generous. It was a Greek term used for judges who did not press the letter of the law, but sought to be reasonable rather than strict in the application of it. The noun form is used of Christ (2 Cor. 10:1).

The next trait is "reasonable." It carries the idea of being open to reason, yielding to persuasion. Such a person is open to other ideas and willing to learn from others rather than be close-minded and stubborn. "Full of mercy" suggests an active concern for the suffering, more than just a feeling of pity. The God of mercy deals with us in mercy (2:13; Ps. 86:5; Eph. 2:4) and desires mercy to be exercised among His children (Isa. 58:6-7; Matt. 5:7). Wisdom from above is also full of "good fruits." That refers to practical acts of kindness. True mercy results in a rich harvest of deeds, not just sympathetic feelings.

The term *unwavering* is used only here in the New Testament. The Greek word is formed of the term "divide" with the negative prefix, meaning literally "undivided." It carries one of two meanings. If taken passively, it means "unwavering, unvacillating, single-minded, constant." The participle without the negative prefix is used in this manner in 1:6, and translated "doubting." In the active sense, though, it means "without making distinctions, without partiality" (cf. the verb form without the negative prefix in 2:4, "made distinctions"). Either meaning is possible in the context; true wisdom is unwavering and is also without partiality. The final characteristic is "without hypocrisy." It carries the idea of being genuine, without pretense—being sincere. Heavenly wisdom does not hide under a mask. Paul said the same of love. It also must be unhypocritical (Rom. 12:9; cf. 1 Pet. 1:22).

In contrast to earthbound wisdom, which results in disorder and various kinds of evil, heavenly wisdom results in righteousness and peace (v. 18). The link between that verse and previous verses is the concept of peace. Earthly wisdom brings strife; heavenly wisdom is peace loving. The usual relationship between righteousness and peace is that of cause and effect; the result of righteousness is peace. There is "the peaceful fruit of righteousness" (Heb. 12:11; cf. Isa. 32:17). James seems to reverse that order, however, and makes peace foundational to righteousness.

Righteousness here should be thought of as acts of

righteousness, much like 1:20, "The anger of man does not achieve the righteousness of God." "Peace" is the fertile soil in which righteousness can blossom. "The seed whose fruit is righteousness" is better translated "the harvest [fruit] of righteousness" (RSV, NASB margin). It could be understood either as the "fruit which is righteousness" or the "fruit which comes from righteousness." The former meaning would speak of righteousness being a crop, the resultant produce (NEB, NIV, RSV). The other meaning is that the fruit that springs from righteousness is the seed that is sown to produce more harvest (KJV, NASB). To understand righteousness as the fruit is the preferred meaning. The NIV renders the verse: "Peacemakers who sow in peace raise a harvest of righteousness."

The fruit is sown "in peace," which speaks of the condition in which righteousness can flourish. Surely righteousness cannot be produced when conditions are full of strife, jealousy, and selfishness. The phrase "by those who make peace" may also be rendered "for those who make peace." Either makes good sense. The fruit of righteousness is both to be enjoyed by peacemakers, as well as be sown by them. The picture James portrays is that of a field where the peacemakers, those who exercise wisdom from above, sow their gracious deeds with the resulting harvest of righteousness. That harvest is in bold contrast to those who sow jealousy and strife. Those with heavenly wisdom seek to reconcile people and bring harmony in the body. Though this entire chapter has primarily the teacher in mind, each member of the body has the responsibility of promoting peace and righteousness. No official position is necessary to advance unity in the body.

8

GIVING GOD FIRST PRIORITY

James 4:1-10

The sudden mention of "quarrels and conflicts" is a startling change from the tranquil picture of peace and righteousness just portrayed. The wisdom from above was shown to be characterized by various godly virtues (3:17), but wisdom from below produces many negative results (3:16). The basic cause for those negative outgrowths, such as disorder, jealousy, strife, and other evils, is now given. The primary cause is a love for self rather than God; a friendship with the world and not with God. The Christian must give God first place in his life. The worldly man is self-centered; the godly man is God-centered. This paragraph can be divided into three sections: the results of giving self first priority (vv. 1-3), the error of establishing wrong priorities (vv. 4-6), and finally, the requirement of giving God first priority (vv. 7-10).

THE RESULTS OF GIVING SELF FIRST PRIORITY (4:1-3)

Using his characteristic question-answer method, James introduces this new paragraph with a question, which is immediately answered. Though he does not use the characteristic "brethren" at this point, its use in verse 11 suggests that he is speaking to Christians, Christians who are struggling with worldliness and selfishness, resulting in conflict in the body. Paul addressed the same problem when he wrote of the conflict between the flesh and the Spirit (Gal. 5:17-24; cf. Rom. 7:23; 1 Pet. 2:11). With two direct questions, one building on the other, James isolates the source of the conflict. The first question is diagnostic—"what" (*pothen,* lit. "from where," "whence")—and in the second question the readers are challenged to admit his diagnosis. The adverb is given before each noun, adding emphasis (lit., "whence quarrels and whence conflicts"). Both nouns, "quarrels and conflicts," are in the plural, indicating that they were not isolated events, but a continuing problem in their midst. The two terms are nearly synonymous, but if a distinction is made, the first refers to a continuing state of hostility and the second to specific outbursts of enmity and antagonism.

"Among you" could be rendered "in you," and thus refer to inner personal struggles and tensions; but it more probably speaks of the conflicts within the church body. The two ideas, though, cannot be completely detached, for external conflicts often expose inner struggles. A person not at peace with himself can surely not be at peace with his associates. By using the pronoun "you," James separates himself from those who are causing discord in the body.

Moralists have often asked about the source of human discord, but seldom have they been willing to point the finger at the real cause. In the second question, James asks his readers to acknowledge that the source of human conflict is in man himself. The "source" (*ek;* lit., "out of") of the disturbances is one's pleasures. The source is not environmental but is an inner problem. "Pleasures" (*hedōnōn*) is the term from which we get the word *hedonism.* It refers to a self-seeking philosophy, a philosophy wherein pleasure is the summum bonum of life. The "If it feels good, do it" way of life is an example. Jesus, in the parable of the sower, spoke of the "pleasures" of life choking the good seed so that no fruit was produced (Luke 8:14). Those "pleasures" are enslaving (Titus 3:3; cf. 2 Pet. 2:13).

That desire for pleasure wages relentless war in our members. "Wage war" continues the imagery of conflict and battle. Worldly pleasures are portrayed as soldiers in battle out to win. Peter wrote of "fleshly lusts, which wage war against the soul" (1 Pet. 2:11). The phrase "in your members," like the earlier phrase "among you," may refer either to the personal life of the individual or to the members of the community. Again, those two possible interpretations go hand in hand, for individuals who have not been victorious over the sinful cravings of the flesh will inevitably be in conflict with other members in the body. When sinful pleasures gain the dominance in a person, that individual will become a center of strife in the Christian community.

Pleasure never gives full satisfaction, life remains unsatisfied, and the thirst for more remains unquenched. That cycle becomes the emphasis of verses 2-3. The punctuation of the first part of verse 2 is uncertain, therefore translations vary. Many translations, such as the NASB, NEB, and RSV, punctuate it in such a way as to have two parallel statements:

> You lust and do not have: you murder.
> You covet and cannot obtain: you fight and quarrel.

Others, such as ASV, KJV, NIV, suggest, "You lust and have not: you kill and desire to have and cannot obtain: you fight and war." Davids suggests the following structure:

> You lust
>   and you do not have
> you kill and envy
>   and you are not able to obtain
> you fight and quarrel
>   [and] you do not have because you do not ask
> you ask
>   and you do not receive because . . . .[1]

If the first punctuation is used (and this seems probable), the last verb in each couplet suggests a resultant act: "You lust and do not have, so you murder." Murdering, fighting, and quarreling are results of unsatisfied lust and envy—results of thwarted desires. The object of lust is not mentioned, but in the context it relates closely to "pleasures" (v. 1). Satisfaction through self-gratification is elusive. The insatiable drive for more leads to murder. David's lust for

---

1. Davids, 157-58.

Bathsheba led to Uriah's death (2 Sam. 11:2-17), and Ahab's covetousness led to Naboth's murder (1 Kings 21:1-13). It is out of the heart of man that murder springs (Mark 7:21). James is probably using "murder" in a figurative sense much like he spoke of "conflicts" (v. 1). John spoke of those who hated as murderers (1 John 3:15). In like manner Jesus taught that to be angry with a brother is to kill (Matt. 5:21-22). Through jealousy and strife one can destroy a brother's reputation.

Adamson suggests that the verb "you commit murder" does not fit the passage, therefore it is "best to change the text from 'you kill' (*phoneuete*) to 'you are envious' (*phthoneite*)."[2] Moffatt gives this translation: "You crave, and miss what you want: you envy and covet, but you cannot acquire: you wrangle and fight" (cf. Phillips). There is, however, absolutely no textual support for that conjecture.

In the next couplet, the outcome of unsatisfied envy is mentioned: "You fight and quarrel." The individual is frustrated because not only does he "not have," he also "cannot obtain." There is an inability to get. That inability causes frustrations that lead to all kinds of tensions in the body, such as fighting and quarreling. "Fight" and "quarrel" are the verb forms, in reverse order, of the nouns "quarrels" and "conflicts" (v. 1).

Two reasons are assigned for not having a satisfied life. First, some do not have because they do not ask (v. 2); and second, some ask, but they ask with wrong motives (v. 3). A satisfied life can only come from God. To attempt to satisfy our deepest yearnings through worldly pleasure leads to frustrations and conflict. God, the giver of good and perfect gifts (1:17), is the one who should be pursued, not hedonistic pleasures. Moses chose "rather to endure ill-treatment with the people of God, than to enjoy the passing pleasures of sin; considering the reproach of Christ greater riches than the treasures of Egypt" (Heb. 11:25-26). True satisfaction comes

---

2. Adamson, 168.

not through the pursuit of pleasures, but in asking from God. "Ask" is in the present tense, suggesting that there had been a repeated failure to ask. James has earlier mentioned that asking must be done in faith (1:5-6).

So some had failed to ask, but others had asked with wrong motives (v. 3). They too had not received. "You ask with wrong motives" is literally "You ask wrongly" (*kakōs*). Scripture gives several qualifications for answered prayer: one must ask in faith (1:6), without doubting (1:6), in Jesus' name (John 16:24), according to God's will (1 John 5:14), while in right relationship with others (1 Pet. 3:7), and when there is no iniquity in the heart (Ps. 66:18). James is writing to those who have their own selfish ends in view when they pray. They are not necessarily praying for sinful things, but rather they are praying out of self-seeking motives. The Christian must continually evaluate his prayer life to make certain that his prayers spring out of a desire for God's glory and not from self-interest.

THE ERROR OF ESTABLISHING WRONG PRIORITIES (4:4-6)

Having exposed the barrenness of selfish priorities, James issues a sharp rebuke to those who have wrong priorities. He bases his rebuke on two factors: one cannot be faithful to God and the world at the same time, for the two are diametrically opposed to each other (v. 4), and God through His Spirit indwelling the believer gives the necessary dynamic to follow through with the right priority of wholehearted devotion to God (vv. 5-6).

"You adulteresses" (some translations read "adulterers and adulteresses," KJV) comes as an abrupt rebuke to those who are making pleasures the chief end of life. Adultery is a common Old Testament figure of Israel's unfaithfulness to God (Deut. 31:16; Ezek. 16; Hosea 9:1). To depart from the true God is expressed as spiritual adultery, a breaking of the marriage vows. Jesus spoke of "an evil and adulterous generation" (Matt. 12:39). Both God and the world are wooing the human heart. The longing for pleasure leads to disobedience and rejection of God. "Friendship" (*philia*) with the world has as a result enmity with God. Paul wrote of those who were "lovers of pleasure [*philēdonoi*] rather than lovers of God [*philotheoi*]" (2 Tim. 3:4). Jesus also taught concerning the incongruity of divided loyalties: "No servant can serve two masters; for either he will hate the one, and love the other, or else he will hold to one, and despise the other. You cannot serve God and mammon" (Luke 16:13). Neutrality is impossible. Either the mind is set on the flesh or on the Spirit (Rom. 8:5-8). The conclusion is clear. When one seeks the friendship of the world, the inevitable result is that he makes himself an enemy of God. The individual has made a deliberate choice to give allegiance to the world and its alluring pleasures. Abraham made the right choice and "he was called the friend [*philos*] of God" (2:23).

The next verses (vv. 5-6) give the scriptural support for what has just been said. Several problems of interpretation must be addressed. The first relates to the source of the seeming quotation: "He jealously desires the Spirit which He has made to dwell in us." That statement is not found verbatim in the Old Testament, so several solutions have been proposed. One is that James is quoting some unknown Greek translation. Another solution is that the last half of verse 5 and the first half of verse 6 are parenthetical, and the actual citation is from Proverbs 3:34, quoted in the last half of verse 6. A third possibility is to interpret the first part of verse 5 as applying to what had preceded: Scripture was not spoken in vain that friendship with the world is enmity with God. That would mean that the last half of verse 5 is not a quotation, but rather a continuation of the argument. Yet another solution is that James is making an inexact citation, a paraphrase, of some Old Testament passage, such as Exodus 20:5. Still others have suggested that James is summarizing the thought of several Old Testament passages without intending to make a verbatim quotation (cf. Gen. 6:3, 6; Deut. 32:21; Isa. 63:8-16; Zech. 8:2). A simple solution, and perhaps the best, is to make verse 5 two independent sentences, the first a question and the second an affirmation: "Do you think that the Scripture speaks to no purpose? He jealously desires the Spirit which He has made to dwell in us." That avoids the need to find a direct citation from the Old Testament. James tells his readers that Scripture does not speak in vain as it addresses the issue of friendship (v. 4), nor does it communicate in vain as it speaks to the issue that follows (vv. 5*b*-6).

The question asked (v. 5*a*) should receive a negative reply: "No, Scripture does *not* speak to no purpose." "No purpose" is literally "in vain." The probing question is, "Does Scripture have an authoritative claim on our lives, or is it a hollow, empty claim?" The authority of Scripture is the issue at hand.

The second half of verse 5 also presents difficulties for the translator and the interpreter. Several matters must be clarified. First, the word "spirit" (*pneuma*) may refer either to the Holy Spirit or the human spirit. Second, that term may be either the subject or the object of the verb. Third, the phrase "jealously desires" may be used either in a good or a bad sense. And fourth, the manuscripts are divided on the verb "has made to dwell," some reading simply "dwells" (cf. DV, KJV). The reading "has made to dwell" has better manuscript support and is followed by most modern translations. Assuming that is the correct reading, there are still several variations of translation possible.

1. "The Spirit which He [God] has made to dwell in us jealously desires" (Berkeley, NASB margin, NIV margin). In other words, the Holy Spirit given us by God longs for our undivided loyalty.
2. "The spirit which He [God] has made to dwell in us jealously desires" (ASV, DV, KJV, NEB, NIV). In this translation, man's spirit, given him by God (Gen. 2:7; Isa. 42:5), desires evil things.
3. "He [God] jealously desires the Spirit which He has made to dwell in us" (NASB). Here one member of the Trinity is described as longing for another member. The Father's love for the Son is often expressed; here it is the Father's love for the Spirit.
4. "He [God] jealously desires the spirit which He has made

dwell in us'' (NIV margin). Somewhat similar to number one, this meaning expresses God's longing for our spirit's undivided loyalty.

Solutions number one or four seem the most likely; both two and three seem out of context. God is jealous for the loyalties of His people. Whether it is expressed as God's being desirous for our spirit or as the indwelling Spirit's being jealous for us, the effect is nearly identical. If the reference is to the Holy Spirit, and it seems it is, this is the only place in the epistle where He is mentioned. The yearning of the Spirit is in keeping with Paul's description of the battle raging between the flesh and the Spirit (Gal. 5:17).

The term ''desires'' suggests a strong, longing affection. ''Jealously'' can be used in either a good or a bad sense. If it is a bad sense, then we have man tending toward envy; but if in a good sense, God is desiring man and jealous for his affections. Scripture speaks of God as a jealous God (Ex. 20:5). He does not want to share our affection with the world. If that interpretation is correct, God's Spirit is shown to be a jealous lover. He longs for our affection. Such an idea suits the context well. Some, however, feel that the context of verse 6 argues for solution two. The grace of God is yet ''greater in comparison with the strength of the evil spirit in man.''[3]

God, being a jealous God, makes rigorous requirements of allegiance, but He also provides the necessary grace to give the demanded loyalty (v. 6). As the Spirit of God yearns for our undivided loyalty, while at the same time the allurements of the world seek our attention, God continues to give additional grace. In light of the preceding verses, the ''he'' may refer to either the Father, the giver of the Spirit, or to the Spirit Himself. Perhaps no clear distinction should be made. God has been mentioned as the generous giver of wisdom (1:5) and the one who provides every good and perfect gift, including salvation (1:17-18). Now He is portrayed as the giver of grace, the one who ''gives grace to the humble.'' To

3. Ibid., 173.

Paul He said, "My grace is sufficient for you" (2 Cor. 12:9).

The comparative "greater" may mean "more and more grace" or "abundant grace." Because it is comparative, there must be some point of comparison: greater grace than what? Perhaps it is grace greater than the power of evil (cf. v. 7). God has promised necessary grace in time of need (Heb. 4:16). Paul stated, "Where sin increased, grace abounded all the more" (Rom. 5:20).

James continues with a quotation from Proverbs 3:34, "God is opposed to the proud, but gives grace to the humble" (cf. 1 Pet. 5:5). The unexpressed subject of "says" is either Scripture ("it"), or God ("He"). The meaning is essentially the same. God is the author of Scripture, and for Scripture to speak is for God to speak. The one who defiantly rejects God's rightful claim on his life, God will oppose; but to the one who humbly submits to His sovereignty, God will give grace. He will provide gracious forgiveness for the past and enablement for the future. In the context, the proud are those who are friends of this world, seeking the pleasures it has to offer. The humble are those who recognize their insufficiencies and give absolute allegiance to God. The quotation from Proverbs sets the stage for the commands that follow.

THE REQUIREMENT OF GIVING GOD FIRST PRIORITY (4:7-10)

Having expressed the serious error of friendship with the world, James provides the solution to rectify the problem in a series of ten imperatives. These are practical exhortations to make God the first priority, rather than making pleasure the summum bonum of life. Each of the commands is in the aorist tense, suggesting urgency and decisive action.

The first imperative, "submit," is a general command that introduces what is to follow. It speaks of voluntary subordination to God. One can obey without true subordination and humility, but a readiness to submit to another is a sign of true humility. God does not seek forced obedience; He desires voluntary allegiance and devotion. Submission is a key concept in the Christian life. Christians are to be subject to secular government (1 Pet. 2:13), wives to their own husbands (1 Pet. 3:1), younger people to the elderly (1 Pet. 5:5), servants to masters (Titus 2:9), and believers one to another (Eph. 5:21). Someday all creation will be brought into subordination to God (1 Cor. 15:27).

The other side of submitting to God is to "resist the devil." The Greek word translated "devil" means "slanderer." The Septuagint uses it almost uniformly for the Hebrew term rendered *Satan,* meaning "accuser." The believer is called upon to resist him, a military metaphor meaning "take your stand against." The same imperative is used in 1 Peter 5:8-9, where we are also exhorted to "resist" the devil. In that passage Satan is given the epithet "your adversary," and he is described as prowling "about like a roaring lion, seeking someone to devour." According to Peter, our resistance must be done in faith. The devil also has his militia of evil forces whom we must "resist in the evil day" (Eph. 6:13). Satan, as a deceitful schemer (Eph. 6:11), may come disguised as "an angel of light" (2 Cor. 11:14) or a "roaring lion" (1 Pet. 5:8; cf. "dragon," Rev. 12:9). He is seeking to build his kingdom by subverting the people of God into changing their allegiance.

A comforting promise is added to the imperative: "He will flee from you." When one takes a stand against Satan and his hosts, Satan will make a hasty retreat. Jesus, the author of our salvation (Heb. 2:10), was victorious over Satan in life (Matt. 4:1-11) and in death (John 12:31); because of that victory Satan has been rendered powerless (Heb. 2:14). Through Christ's victory, those in Christ can be victorious. The Christian is called upon to be strong in the Lord and equip himself with the whole armor of God (Eph. 6:10-17), and then by faith put the enemy to flight. It is noteworthy that the command to resist Satan and the promised victory is not an isolated command; rather, it occurs between two imperatives: "Submit to God" and "Draw near to God." It is only as the believer obeys those commands that he is able to put Satan to flight by resisting him.

Not only are we to submit to God as a servant to his master, but we are also to "draw near to God" (v. 8) as a worshiper entering into communion with God. The verb "draw near" is used often of the Levitical priest approaching God with the various sacrifices (Ex. 19:22; Lev. 10:3) and of individuals coming to God in worship (Hos. 12:6). It is through the new high priesthood of Jesus Christ that the Christian can "draw near to God" (Heb. 7:19). With that imperative there is also a following promise, "He will draw near to you." Communion and fellowship go both ways—we have fellowship with God, and He with us (Rev. 3:20).

To worship God properly, preparations must be made. In the Levitical system, the priests went through the ritual of washing before they could take up their various ceremonial responsibilities (Ex. 30:19-21). So also the penitent. For him to approach God, he needs a cleansing. In characteristic Hebrew poetic style, James gives two parallel imperatives:

> Cleanse your hands, you sinners; and
> purify your hearts, you double-minded.

David wrote that it is those who have "clean hands and a pure heart" who may ascend to the hill of the Lord and stand in His holy place (Ps. 24:3-4; cf. Isa. 1:16). The truth of spiritual cleansing was symbolically portrayed and verbally communicated by our Lord to Peter and the rest of His disciples as He began to wash their feet (John 13:3-17, especially vv. 5-10). Both hands and heart are defiled and need purging. The term *hands* is used symbolically of outward deeds, for the hands are instruments used to perform acts of a defiling, evil nature. The *heart* speaks of the inner life. It is out of the heart, the inner life, that evil thoughts and acts proceed (Mark 7:21-23). Peter wrote that since his readers had purified their souls, they were now "fervently [to] love one another from the heart" (1 Pet. 1:22). A purified heart and clean hands cannot be separated. A godly life-style will flow from a pure heart. The appearance of seemingly clean hands without a pure heart is hypocrisy and a sham.

The readers are addressed as "sinners" and "double-minded.'' Though James is addressing Christians, they were Christians who by seeking the pleasures of the world had not established the right priority of wholehearted devotion to God. They were sinners in that they were not living up to God's standards; they were double-minded in that they had divided loyalties, desiring the world while also seeking to please God (cf. Matt. 6:24). ''Double-minded'' (used in 1:8) may also suggest a struggle in the mind between the heart and the hands: knowing what is right in the heart, but not doing it with the hands. Hiebert states succinctly, ''God demands undivided affection as well as undefiled conduct.''[4]

The two parallel imperatives for cleansing are followed by a triplet of terse commands: ''Be miserable and mourn and weep'' (v. 9). Sin is serious business, and the call for cleansing must not be taken in a casual, light-hearted, or frivolous manner. ''Be miserable'' is the verb form of the adjective used by Paul when he recognized his helplessness in the face of the power of sin in his members: ''Wretched man that I am!'' (Rom. 7:24). Some have thought that that means ''make yourself wretched,'' in the sense of practicing some type of asceticism or self-castigation. It is better understood, however, as having an inner feeling of shame and misery because of sin. The realization of the sinfulness of sin produces a sense of wretchedness.

The last two commands in the triplet, ''mourn and weep,'' express the outworking of the inner feelings of misery. Those two terms, which occur often together (cf. Luke 6:25), are roughly synonymous. In the Beatitudes Matthew records, ''Blessed are those who mourn'' (5:4), and Luke has, ''You who weep'' (6:21). Mourning is the outward expression of deep grief, indicating an intense hurt that cannot be easily disguised. Weeping is the tearful expression of mourning.

Evidently the pursuit of pleasure had been filled with hilarity and light-hearted gaity; therefore James urges, ''Let your laughter be turned into mourning, and your joy to gloom.''

---

4. Hiebert, 264.

Laughter in itself is not sin (Psalm 126:2), but the flippant laughter of unconcern and self-satisfaction should rather be turned to mourning. And further, the superficial joy experienced in worldly pleasures should be reversed to gloom. "Gloom" speaks of a downcast appearance due to a heavy heart. It suggests dejection because of shame. True joy is a fruit of the Spirit (Gal. 5:22), rejoicing is commanded (Phil. 4:4), but the irresponsible frivolous joy of temporal pleasure is not to be considered proper Christian behavior. Moses chose not "to enjoy the passing pleasures of sin" (Heb. 11:25).

The final imperative in the series is "Humble yourselves in the presence of the Lord" (v. 10). That completes the circle, bringing the thought back to the starting point: God "gives grace to the humble" (v. 6). The verb "humble" could be passive or middle, either "be humbled" or "humble yourself." Clearly the thought is voluntary humiliation. In the presence of the Lord a man must acknowledge and deplore his utter unworthiness. By using "Lord," James reminds the reader that there is a heavenly Master in whose presence and under whose watchful eye he stands. In similar fashion Peter writes, "Humble yourselves, therefore, under the mighty hand of God" (1 Pet. 5:6; cf. Matt. 18:4). As with two previous imperatives (vv. 7-8), there is a promise attached to the command "He will exalt you." The way to exaltation is humility. Jesus reminded His listeners, "Everyone who exalts himself shall be humbled, and he who humbles himself shall be exalted" (Luke 14:11; cf. Matt. 23:12). Self-exaltation leads to ruin; humility brings divine exaltation. To be truly significant one must not seek after the pleasures of this world; but one must make his first priority whole-hearted, devoted allegiance to God. God has promised to honor such a person.

9

AVOIDING PRESUMPTUOUS BEHAVIOR

JAMES 4:11-17

Human pride and self-exaltation often lead to the disparagement of others and presumptuous behavior. When one humbles himself and submits to God, his attitude toward his Christian brothers and sisters and toward life in general will make a marked change. The spirit of humility cannot coexist with a spirit of haughtiness toward others and overconfidence in the security and invulnerability of the future. Having established the need to give God undivided allegiance (4:1-10), James proceeds to write against censorious and judgmental speech within the body and overconfidence in the future. The section can be divided into three parts: the inappropriateness of presumptuous judging (vv. 11-12), the foolishness of presumptuous planning (vv. 13-15), and the evil of a presumptuous attitude (vv. 16-17).

THE INAPPROPRIATENESS OF PRESUMPTUOUS JUDGING (4:11-12)

The connection between these verses and the preceding is obvious. When true humility is lacking, malicious backbiting will often occur. The imperatives of verse 7-10 are Godward; the emphasis now is manward. James again returns to the topic of human speech (cf. 1:26; 2:12; 3:1-12). The command "Do not speak against" is present tense, indicating that censorious speech was habitual among the readers. It needed to be terminated. "To speak against" (lit., "to speak down on") carries the idea of running someone down, to lower a person in someone else's estimation. Often the motive is to exalt oneself by maliciously slandering another. Peter writes on non-Christians speaking down against Christians (1 Pet. 2:12; 3:16). That is to be expected; but for a Christian to do it to a fellow believer is inappropriate, irresponsible, and a usurpation of God's prerogative to judge. The reciprocal pronoun "one another" suggests that the situation was not one-sided, but those being maligned were themselves slandering in return. There was a failure to turn the other cheek. What makes that so grave is that they were "brethren." Members within the family of God were running each other down. Brothers and sisters "for whom Christ died" (Rom. 14:15) were being hurt. The law of love was being violated. Small wonder that there were quarrels and conflicts going on in the body!

Having given the injunction against abusive speech, James proceeds to explain why such verbal disparagement of a fellow Christian is so inappropriate. Such a person sets himself up as a judge of the law (v. 11), arrogantly usurping God's prerogative to be the Lawgiver and Judge (v. 12). The one who speaks against a brother is, in effect, passing judgment on his peer. The command of the Lord is "Do not pass judgment and you will not be judged; and do not condemn, and you shall not be condemned; pardon, and you will be pardoned" (Luke 6:37; cf. Matt. 7:1). Paul counseled, "Let us not judge one another any more" (Rom. 14:13). To disparage a brother, then, is placed by James on the level of unauthorized judging and malicious discrediting of a brother. So serious and unfamilylike is the matter that James used "brother" or "brethren" three times in this one verse.

To be a judge over a brother's conduct is to usurp the privileges of deity and pass judgment on divine law. "Law" should not be thought of as the Mosaic law with all its ordinances, but rather the heart of God's moral law—perfect love to God and one's neighbor (Lev. 19:18; Deut. 6:5; Mark 12:30-31; Gal. 5:14). Here the emphasis is on the second part—love to one's neighbor—already identified as the ''perfect law, the law of liberty'' (1:25) and the ''royal law'' (2:8). To backbite and run one another down is to violate the divine law of love. In doing that one is, in effect, implying that the law is not right and should be annulled. In the original Old Testament context of the command to love one's neighbor (Lev. 19:18), several related commands are mentioned: ''You are to judge your neighbor fairly'' (v. 15); ''You shall not go about as a slanderer among your people'' (v. 16); ''You shall not hate your fellow-countryman in your heart'' (v. 17); and ''You shall not take vengeance, nor bear any grudge against the sons of your people'' (v. 18). Thus grudging, slandering, backbiting, and unfairness all violate the law of love. And to violate a law is tantamount to judging the law and putting oneself above it. As James writes, ''You are not a doer of the law, but a judge of it.'' By disregarding the law, one is implying that he is qualified to abrogate it and enact a different or better law. God wants believers to be doers, not merely hearers (1:23; cf. Rom. 2:13), or worse yet, judges of the law.

It is not fitting for a brother to become a judge, for ''there is only one Lawgiver and Judge'' (v. 12). ''One'' can be understood either as the subject of the verb ''is'' (''one [only] is the Lawgiver and Judge''), or as the predicate nominative (''there is [only] one Lawgiver and Judge''). The former rendering emphasizes the uniqueness of the one who is the Lawgiver and Judge; the second emphasizes the truth of monotheism. God gave the law; He, who is the only God, is the only one above the law. To seek to change or abrogate the law is to seek to take the place of God.

God, not man, ''is able to save and to destroy.'' That twofold capacity affirming God's sovereignty is a truth often expressed in Scripture: ''It is I who put to death and give life'' (Deut. 32:39; cf. 2 Kings 5:7). ''Is able'' emphasizes that God is fully able to carry out His purposes. Often in Scripture the believer is comforted, knowing that God is able (Matt. 3:9; Rom. 14:4; Eph. 3:20). ''Save'' and ''destroy'' may have present application, but the eschatological meaning seems to be primarily in view. It is then that God will give His verdict as the sovereign judge.

James concludes his argument concerning inappropriate judging with the penetrating question "But who are you who judge your neighbor?" It is as if he is saying, "Who are you to take God's place?" In the original, "you" is in the position of emphasis. It makes the question personal and piercing: "You, who are you who judge your neighbor?" "Neighbor" replaces "brother," indicating clearly that the subject is the "royal law" of loving one's neighbor (2:8).

THE FOOLISHNESS OF PRESUMPTUOUS PLANNING (4:13-15)

These verses contain another example of man's arrogance and self-sufficiency. In the previous section James addressed the inappropriateness and arrogance of assuming to oneself God's role as judge; now he turns to address the arrogant attitude of self-sufficiency in presumptuous planning. Man often assumes he is the final arbitrator of his own life; he should rather walk humbly before God and trust in His providential care. But man easily gets so engrossed in the pursuit of financial gain that he fails to take God into consideration in his planning. In this section, James first gives a brief statement reflecting presumption in planning for the future (v. 13), then shows the foolishness of such an attitude (v. 14), followed by a correct approach toward the future (v. 15).

"Come now" (cf. 5:1) introduces a change in the subject matter. Itinerant business people who have been successful in merchandising are now addressed. The picture of an itinerant merchant fits will the Jewish business person of the Roman world. Lydia, "a seller of purple fabrics," went from Thyatira to Philippi (Acts 16:14), and Priscilla and Aquila moved with their trade from place to place (Acts 18:1-2, 18). James's rebuke is not against planning for the future; it is against planning without taking God into account.

Evidently the past successes in commercial enterprises gave the merchants James is addressing confidence in their ability to make even more money. In discussing their plans, they treated the future as if they had control over it and it was their property. They had planned the time of departure, the city to be visited, the time to be spent, the business to be transacted, and the profit to be made, all without taking into consideration the providential working of God. Scripture warns, "Do not boast about tomorrow, for you do not know what a day may bring forth" (Prov. 27:1). In the parable of the rich fool, the rich man made plans for a secure future without considering that the length of his life was not within his power to determine (Luke 12:16-21).

By exposing the foolishness of their presumptuous attitude toward the future, James lays bare two weaknesses in their thinking: they were assuming the events of tomorrow, when in reality no human knows what tomorrow holds; and they were not taking into consideration the transitoriness and uncertainty of human life. There might not even be a tomorrow.

Translations vary on the punctuation of the first part of verse 14. It may be taken as two sentences: "Yet you do not know what shall be on the morrow. What is your life?" (NEB, NIV, RSV). Or it may be rendered as one: "Yet you do not know what your life will be like tomorrow" (NASB). The former suggests that for one to assume that he will even be alive on the morrow is presumptuous. The latter rendering assumes the person will be alive on the morrow, but to know what that day will bring forth is presumptuous. In either case the emphasis is that we do not know about tomorrow, whether we will even be here, let alone be certain of our man-made plans.

The proof of that is that life is but a "vapor." Different terms are used in Scripture of the brevity of human life, such as "breath" (Job 7:7), "cloud" (Job 7:9), "grass" (Ps. 103:15), and "lengthened shadow" (Ps. 102:11). *Vapor* is a term used for a "puff of smoke," "steam" rising from hot water, or "breath" coming from the nostrils on a cold day. It is an apt description of something that has very little permanence. There is a play on words; literally, "appearing and then disappearing," emphasizing the transient and short-lived nature of life. Hiebert concludes, "How foolish therefore to ignore the unchanging God and then proudly plan for their life that is as fleeting as a wisp of vapor!"[1]

Rather than presumptuous planning, one ought in humility to take God into account in planning for the future (v. 15). This verse brings the reader back to and is in contrast with verse 13. Instead of the arrogant talking of verse 13, the pious person ought to say, "If the Lord wills." Ropes labels that "a true expression of Christian submission to divine providence."[2] The formula "If the Lord wills" is an aorist subjunctive: "If the Lord should will." It leaves the situation indefinite and does not presume upon God's prerogative to will as He chooses. Several times the apostles used that expression as they planned the future (Acts 18:21; 1 Cor. 4:19; cf. 16:7). Where the formula is not used (Acts 19:21), certainly the apostles assumed it in their attitude toward the future. Though the phrase "God willing" (*deo volente* [D.V.]) can degenerate, and often has, into mere hypocrisy and empty piety, it should not deter the humble Christian from expressing his dependence on God verbally and otherwise.

God's providential control is over both our lives and our actions: "We shall live and also do this or that." To plan ahead is biblical; not to plan is foolish. But planning must be approached from the standpoint of God's will. Careful forethought is not depreciated, but the attitude of haughty self-confidence and independence from God is exposed.

THE EVIL OF A PRESUMPTUOUS ATTITUDE (4:16-17)

"But as it is" turns the attention to the present corrupt attitude they had. The basic evil displayed is that of presumptuous arrogance. "Boast" can have either a good or a bad

1. Hiebert, 277.
2. James Hardy Ropes, *A Critical and Exegetical Commentary on the Epistle of St. James,* The International Critical Commentary, ed. Alfred Plummer and Francis Brown (Edinburgh: T. & T. Clark, 1978), 280.

sense. In 1:9 it is used in a good sense (cf. Gal. 6:14; Phil. 3:3); here in a bad sense (cf. 1 Cor. 1:29; Gal. 6:13). The condescending backbiting of verse 11 and the planning of verse 15 is, in effect, evil boasting. Their boasting finds expression in their "arrogance," which is in the plural and carries the idea of insolence and of pretentious bragging. In 1 John 2:16 the term is used in company with "lust": "The lust of the flesh and the lust of the eyes and the boastful pride of life." Those worldly attitudes are further stated by John as not having their source from the Father, but from the world. Such boasting with its accompanying pretentious bragging "is evil." It has satanic characteristics, for Satan is called "the evil one" (Eph. 6:16; cf. Matt. 6:13 margin). Because "the whole world lies in the power of the evil one" (1 John 5:19), it is small wonder that worldliness exhibiting itself in arrogant boastfulness is said to be evil.

The concluding maxim caps what has been said: "Therefore, to one who knows the right thing to do, and does not do it, to him it is sin" (v. 17). That verse, which clinches what has been said in the paragraph (vv. 13-17), can be seen as "a general summing up and moral of what has been said before"[3] as far back as 1:22, and provides a bridge to the next section. Emphasis is laid not so much on active wrongdoing, but on the passive failure to do what is right. Paul wrote, "Whatever is not from faith is sin" (Rom. 14:23); John asserted, "Sin is lawlessness" (1 John 3:4), which may mean sin is an active transgression of the law, or, perhaps better, sin is failure to keep the law. Throughout the epistle James has concerned himself with a vibrant, productive faith. The believer who does not produce works of righteousness is actually sinning, and the sin of omission is as serious as the sin of commission. Often it is easier to refrain from committing sins that are forbidden than to perform good at every opportunity afforded. In the parable of the good Samaritan, the Samaritan seized the opportunity to do good, something that

3. Mayor, 152.

the priest and Levite had failed to do (Luke 10:30-35). In the parable of the rich man and Lazarus, the rich man was condemned for his failure to do good toward the needy (Luke 16:19-31). The obligation placed on man is the law of love; any failure in the performance of it is labeled "sin."

The individual addressed is not ignorant of God's requirement to do "right" (*kalon;* lit., "good"). He knows his obligation, but fails to practice it; he is sinning against better knowledge. Micah wrote, "He has told you, O man, what is good; and what does the Lord require of you but to do justice, to love kindness, and to walk humbly with your God?" (6:8). Concerning our obligation, Paul commanded, "Owe nothing to anyone except to love one another; for he who loves his neighbor has fulfilled the law" (Rom. 13:8). It is axiomatic that we more often fail to do the good we ought to do, than actively do what we ought not to do. Arrogance, boasting, and a presumptuous attitude keep us from fulfilling the law of love, therefore they are sin.

10

ENDURING WRONGFUL OPPRESSION

JAMES 5:1-11

"Come now" introduces a new aspect of worldliness: confidence in wealth and the resulting oppression of the poor. Though James is speaking to a new group of people, "you rich," the presumptuous attitude of the traveling merchant (4:13) leads easily into an examination of the oppressive activity of the rich. The first half of this section is a strong rebuke condemning the oppressive rich and his cruel unconcern toward the poor (vv. 1-6); in the second part James turns his attention toward encouraging oppressed believers (vv. 7-11). The oppressive rich are warned of coming judgment, and the believers are encouraged to persevere in spite of unjust treatment.

THE CONDEMNATION OF THE OPPRESSIVE RICH (5:1-6)

"You rich" are those who are wealthy in material things. James is not addressing the rich indescriminately; only those who are acquiring wealth at the expense of the poor (cf. v. 4). Wealth is not in and of itself sinful, but the hoarding of it often creates a false sense of security. The accumulation of it is often accomplished through unjust and sinful means. It is those two dangers related to wealth that Scripture condemns.

The passage does not indicate the religious status of the rich addressed. The rich of 1:9-11 are generally accepted to be members of the believing community, the one of 2:2-3 is evidently a visitor, and those of 2:6 are nonbelievers. Because "brethren" (v. 7) is mentioned in contrast to the rich oppressors, it is generally assumed that James is addressing wealthy individuals outside the Christian church. The words addressed to the rich are meant not primarily for their ears, but as an encouragement to Christians in times of unjust treatment, and to dissuade them from "the folly of setting a high value upon wealth, or of envying those who possess it, or of striving feverishly to obtain it."[1] Though the rich addressed are non-Christians, the wealthy believer is not exempt from the temptations associated with riches (Prov. 30:7-9; 1 Tim. 6:9-10, 17).

The section addressed to the rich can be divided into two parts: the first three verses speak of the coming judgment (vv. 1-3), and the last three verses enumerate three accusations brought against them (vv. 4-6).

At the outset James announces impending judgment: "Weep and howl for your miseries which are coming upon you" (v. 1). That is reminiscent of the Old Testament prophets. Joel wrote, "Awake, drunkards, and weep; and wail, all you wine drinkers" (1:5); and Isaiah in his oracle against Tyre said, "Wail, O ships of Tarshish, for Tyre is destroyed, without house or harbor" (23:1). "Weep," meaning "sob bitterly," was used of wailing for the dead. Scripture records that Peter "wept bitterly" after he realized what he had done in denying Christ (Luke 22:62). Its usage here is not that of a weeping penitent, but of one anguished at the realization of coming judgment. "Howl" is an expression of intense grief. The picture portrayed is that of open and vocal sobbing with howls of agony at the return of Christ in judgment. The self-sufficient rich may appear secure and comfortable in the present life, but when their security is in the uncertainty of riches rather than in the Lord, they will face certain rejection when He comes. Jesus warned, "Woe to you who are rich, for you are receiving your comfort in full" (Luke 6:24).

The rich are called upon to weep and howl because of their "coming" miseries. That speaks of the imminency of the

---

1. R. V. G. Tasker, *The General Epistle of James, The Tyndale New Testament Commentaries,* ed. R. V. G. Tasker (Grand Rapids: Eerdmans, 1980), 16:109-10.

Christ's return (cf. vv. 7, 8, 9). The judgment has not yet come, but it is so certain that it can be spoken of as in the process of coming. "Miseries" speak of wretchedness as the result of calamity coming upon them. The return of the Lord is not a blessed hope for the unbeliever.

In the ancient world there were three signs of wealth: food, clothing, and precious metals. James mentions each of those forms of wealth, with the deterioration coming to each (vv. 2-3*a*). First, "Your riches have rotted." If "riches" is understood in the broad sense of "wealth," then "rotted" should be taken figuratively to mean "become worthless, without value." It is better, however, to understand the riches as referring to perishable foodstuffs, such as grains and oil. In storage those hoarded goods had rotted and become unfit for human consumption. In the parable of the rich fool, the successful, presumptuous farmer who stored up his crops as treasure for himself lost overnight all he had (Luke 12:16-21).

Second, "Your garments have become moth-eaten." In the Near East, richly embroidered garments were recognized as wealth and often used as a medium of exchange. Paul declared, "I have coveted no one's silver or gold or clothes" (Acts 20:33). A moth-eaten garment was practically worthless. Those who amass to themselves an excessive surplus of clothing will awaken to find them filled with ugly holes.

A third form of wealth has also lost its value: "Your gold and your silver have rusted" (v. 3). Because neither silver nor gold actually rust, several suggestions have been advanced concerning the meaning. Some have thought that James, being a poor man and unfamiliar with silver and gold, was ignorant of that fact. That explanation is improbable. Others have suggested that because of the extensive use of alloys in the coins, they did in fact rust. Still others interpret it to mean that the gold and silver would become as valueless as rusted out iron. Most probably James is using "rust" metaphorically of that which destroys and ruins metal and not literally of the oxidizing process of iron. Their gold and silver had become valueless just like their rotted grain and moth-eaten garments. In each of the clauses James uses the perfect tense to describe the judgment that came upon the three forms of wealth. Looking at the wealth from the standpoint of the day of judgment, it was in the state of complete worthlessness. The repeated use of "your" and "you" in those verses keeps the attention focused on the oppressive rich.

The rust that had corroded the wealth of the rich would also bring about their downfall. It would be a "witness" against them and would "consume" their flesh. Rust is a visible sign of the perishableness and transitory nature of riches; it demonstrates the provisional character of all earthly wealth. Further, it portrays the ruin coming on all who put their hope and security in wealth. Covetousness eats into them, destroying them like rust does metal. It is the picture of a festering sore, gnawing away at the flesh. "Like fire" speaks both of the rapidity of destruction and of the excruciating pain. Jesus spoke of the whole body's being cast into Gehenna, a place of unquenchable fire (Matt. 5:29-30; Mark 9:43-48).

Grammatically, "like fire" may be connected either with what goes before or with what follows. If it goes with what follows, the translation is ". . . will consume your flesh, for you have been storing up hell fire." Most translators, though, agree that it should go with what comes before: ". . . consume your flesh like fire." That seems to be the more natural.

The rich have been hoarding up treasures "in the last days." That is an eschatological phrase referring to the period of time before the return of Christ. Since New Testament times Christians have looked for His imminent return, and the church has thought of itself as living in the last days. Peter, quoting Joel, identified the Pentecost experience as being "in the last days" (Acts 2:17; cf. Joel 2:28). He also spoke of mockers coming "in the last days" (2 Pet. 3:3); Paul mentioned difficult times occurring "in the last days" (2 Tim. 3:1), and John declared, "It is the last hour" (1 John 2:18). At a time when people should have been concerned about the imminent return of Christ, the rich were selfishly storing up for themselves perishable treasure, not heeding the warning and counsel of Jesus, "Do not lay up for yourselves treasures upon earth, where moth and rust destroy, and where thieves break in and steal. But lay up for yourselves treasures in heaven, where neither moth nor rust destroys, and where thieves do not break in or steal; for where your treasure is, there will your heart be also" (Matt. 6:19-21).

Having stated their judgment, James now enumerates three charges against them: they have not paid their employees (v. 4), they are living in selfish extravagance (v. 5), and they have gone so far as to murder the righteous (v. 6).

Not paying an employee (v. 4) is a clear violation of Scripture, for "the laborer is worthy of his wages" (1 Tim. 5:18; cf. Matt. 10:10); even an ox while threshing is not to be muzzled (Deut. 25:4). The Old Testament required that a poor man be paid for his work before the sun set (Deut. 24:14-15). The rich man had sufficient food for the present and the immediate future; but the poor man, being on the verge of starvation, needed money at the end of each day to meet that day's needs. In delaying payment the landowner was defrauding his laborers (cf. Jer. 22:13; Mal. 3:5). The "laborers" were "those who did the harvesting." It would perhaps be seen as less serious if James spoke of planters, for then there would be an extended period of time before the crop could be gathered in and sold. But at harvest time, the farmer should be able to pay out of the profits. That he chose not to intensifies the heinousness of the sin against the laborer. What should be a time of joy and thanksgiving because of the plenteous harvest became a time of sadness, oppression, and want for the poor.

Both the withheld money and the defrauded laborers cry out, and God is not deaf to the outcry (cf. Gen. 4:10; Gen. 18:20). "The Lord of Sabaoth" hears the groanings of His people (cf. Ex. 2:24; 6:5). *Sabaoth,* the Hebrew word for "hosts," is used of human armies (Num. 1:3), angelic armies (1 Kings 22:19), and the stars of heaven (Deut. 17:3). The phrase "Lord of Hosts" is one of the majestic titles for God.

He, as the commander of the heavenly host (Josh. 5:15), is the protector of the oppressed. The one who has counted and named all the stars of heaven can also heal the brokenhearted (Ps. 147:3-4).

The rich are further charged with selfish extravagance (v. 5). "Luxuriously" implies a life of selfish luxury. It was lived "on the earth," evidently without regard to the life beyond the grave. In the parable of the rich man, he "habitually dressed in purple and fine linen, gaily living in splendor every day" (Luke 16:19), and was not concerned about the life hereafter. "Wanton pleasure" suggests dissolution or wastefulness. The prodigal in the parable of the prodigal son "squandered his estate with loose living" (Luke 15:13). Paul wrote of the widow "who gives herself to wanton pleasure" (1 Tim. 5:6). Selfish extravagance is not good preparation for meeting the Lord. Using the picture of fattening an animal for slaughter, James vividly explains what the indulgent rich were doing: "You have fattened your hearts in a day of slaughter." The riotous living in which the rich engaged is likened to an ox gorging himself, not realizing that he is actually preparing himself for slaughter.

"Day of slaughter" speaks of the Lord's coming in judgment (Isa. 34:6; Jer. 15:3; Rev. 19:17-18), and is parallel to "the last days" (v. 3). Those people were filling their lives greedily with all kinds of wasteful and worldly pleasures, seemingly oblivious to the imminent day of slaughter.

The third charge concerns murdering the righteous one (v. 6). The oppressive rich used their influence to condemn and kill the righteous. They perverted justice; yet the law says, "You shall not pervert the justice due to your needy brother in his dispute" (Ex. 23:6; cf. Deut. 24:17). Previously James reminded his readers that the rich unbelievers dragged believers into court (2:6); now he goes into more detail. "Put to death" may be taken figuratively, meaning to deprive one of his means of livelihood. Ropes writes, "Oppression which unjustly takes away the means of life is murder."[2] Even

---

2. Ropes, 291.

hatred is murder (1 John 3:15; cf. Matt. 5:21-22). But in light of the context, actual judicial murder seems to be what is meant. That happened to Jesus Christ (Acts 3:14-15) and later to Stephen (Acts 7).

"The righteous man" should be understood not as referring to a specific person, but to righteous men as a class. The righteous man because of his upright behavior stirs up the hatred of the unrighteous rich. Christ is often called the "Righteous One" (Acts 7:52; 1 John 2:1; cf. 1 Pet. 3:18), and some have thought that James is referring to Him. But the context argues for the righteous as a class. Jesus, being perfectly righteous, is the prototype of all those who live righteously. James himself was surnamed the "Just," and he also eventually suffered martyrdom.

The last clause can be understood either as a question or a statement. If it is a question—"Does he not resist you?"—the answer expected would be affirmative. Then the meaning would be prophetic: "Though now his resistance is ineffective, on the day of judgment he will resist them by testifying against them." It is, however, more natural to understand the clause as a statement, either in the sense that the righteous finds himself so overpowered that he is unable to fight back, or that he chooses not to actively oppose his murderers. The latter would be in keeping with the command of Jesus, "Do not resist him who is evil; but whoever slaps you on your cheek, turn to him the other also" (Matt. 5:39), and the injunction of Paul, "Never take your own revenge" (Rom. 12:19). The rich oppressors, rather than using their influence and prestige to champion what was right, chose to make the poor Christian the object of their evil.

AN ENCOURAGEMENT TO THE OPPRESSED BELIEVERS (5:7-11)

In light of the difficult circumstances, the nonresisting Christians needed to be encouraged. That James does along three lines, in each case using the familiar "brethren": first he urges them to be patient in light of the imminent return of Christ, who would correct abuses (vv. 7-8); next he counsels them not to fall into the trap of self-pity and fault-finding, for the Lord is near and He will judge appropriately (v. 9); and finally, the attention of the readers is turned to Old Testament examples so that they could see and appreciate the gracious dealings of the Lord (vv. 10-11).

The verb "be patient" (*makrothumēsate*) carries the idea of "longsuffering." It is commended as a virtue in dealing with difficult and irritating people. God is longsuffering (Rom. 2:4; 9:22; 1 Pet. 3:20; 2 Pet. 3:9), and believers are to be likewise (1 Cor. 13:4; 1 Thess. 5:14). There is another Greek word that also means "to be patient" (*hupomenō*), but in the sense of persevering in the face of difficult circumstances. In the NASB it is often translated "to endure, to persevere" (1:3-4, 12; 5:11). Here the meaning is "to put up" with difficult people. It carries the idea of self-restraint. Just as God is "a gracious and compassionate God, slow to anger and abundant in lovingkindness" (Jonah 4:2; cf. Ps. 86:15), so the believer should be willing to put up with difficult people in trying circumstances. That is not a sign of weakness; rather it demonstrates Christian character. It is an evidence of the Spirit's producing His fruit (Gal. 5:22-23).

The Christian is to patiently endure "until the coming of the Lord," at which time oppression will come to an end. The expression "coming of the Lord," used twice in these two verses, has reference to the personal return of Jesus. The noun "coming" (*parousias*) literally means "being alongside, present." The term may be used of someone's arrival (2 Cor. 7:6) or of someone's presence (Phil. 2:12). When it is used of the second advent, it often emphasizes both the arrival of Christ and His subsequent continuing presence with His people (1 Cor. 15:23; 1 Thess. 4:15; 2 Pet. 1:16; 1 John 2:28). James does not enlarge on the details of Christ's return, but he clearly affirms it as a vital hope of the church, something that should have a sanctifying effect on the body (cf. 2 Pet. 3:11-15; 1 John 3:3).

After giving the command to be patient, James introduces the farmer as an example of patience. He can clear the land, prepare the soil, sow the seed, weed and water the plants, and harvest the crop, but the process of sprouting and growth are beyond the farmer's control. In the parable of the growing seed Christ likened the kingdom of God to a man's planting the seed and harvesting, while the seed itself sprouted, grew, and produced a crop by itself (Mark 4:26-29). Paul wrote of seed being planted and watered by men, but that it is "God who causes the growth" (1 Cor. 3:7). The farmer does his part; then the rest must be left up to the providential workings of God. During the interim between planting and harvesting, the farmer "waits" and is "patient." The verb "waits" carries the idea of waiting expectantly. "Being patient" suggests the attitude of expectancy in spite of uncertainties such as weather and pestilence.

Palestine is dependent on "the early and late rains." The early rains come in late October or early November, and the late rains arrive in late April or May. The early rains provide a moist soil bed where the seed can be sown; the late rains are necessary for the maturing of the crop. The timing of the rain has a direct effect on the size of the crop harvested, and the farmer can only stand back and trust in the providential, timely sending of rain.

As the farmer puts his trust in a reliable God who has established the seasons (Gen. 8:22), so the Christian must wait expectantly and patiently for God (v. 8). In both cases there is confident hope—the farmer is confident of the coming rain, and the Christian of the return of Christ. Two commands are given: the repeated "be patient" and "strengthen your hearts." "Be patient" has the personal pronoun "you" for emphasis. The second command carries the idea of being stouthearted, of establishing one's heart so that it will be firm and resolute. That inner strengthening is sometimes spoken of as the work of God (1 Thess. 3:13; 1 Pet. 5:10), but it is also the responsibility of believers to strengthen other believers (Luke 22:32). Here it is a call for self-strengthening. In spite of the difficult circumstances in which Christians find themselves, they are not to turn to self-pity or complaining, but rather to be patient and have an inner strengthening because "the coming of the Lord is at hand."

The perfect "is at hand," literally meaning "has drawn nigh," denotes imminency. Christ used the same term in "The kingdom of God is at hand" (Mark 1:15); and Peter wrote, "The end of all things is at hand" (1 Pet. 4:7). The assurance that the return of the Christ has drawn nigh is an encouragement to the suffering believer and should have a sanctifying effect on his life (2 Pet. 3:11; 1 John 3:3). That the Lord has delayed His coming (Matt. 25:5) should not cause the Christian to lose hope. His delay is evidence of His grace (2 Pet. 3:9).

Positively, the believer is to be patient; negatively, he is not to "complain" (v. 9). The verb "complain" means "to sigh, to groan" (cf. Mark 7:34; Rom. 8:23). It speaks of sighing because of oppression and difficulties. In trying times it is easy to become impatient and develop feelings and attitudes of criticism and faultfinding. Morale can break down, and small irritations between fellow believers can cause hard feelings. The complainings become reciprocal, "against one another"; and the suppressed critical feelings develop into a form of judging one another, perhaps a lashing out at one another. James warns them to stop the negative feelings, "that you yourselves may not be judged." That echoes the warning of Jesus concerning judging (Matt. 7:1-2). Mutual recrimination in times of stress is hurtful to the body.

Believers must be reminded that there is a higher Judge to which the individual will directly answer (2 Cor. 5:10). The nearness of the supreme Judge is graphically portrayed, "The Judge is standing right at the door." He, standing, ready to push the doors open, can hear what is going on. James is echoing the words of Jesus, "He is near, right at the door" (Mark 13:29). The picture of imminent judgment is as much an incentive to patience as is the coming of Christ to bring deliverance.

Turning back to the positive, James reminds his readers that Old Testament believers also had difficulties. He uses the general example of the Old Testament prophets (v. 10), then the specific example of Job (v. 11). The prohets provide many examples of "suffering and patience." The first term, "suffering," is a compound word meaning "suffering evil, misfortune, or hardship." The second word, "patience," is the noun form of the verb "patient," used earlier in verses 7 and 8. Suffering and patience may be considered as two separate, though connected, items; or the two may form a hendiadys, "patience in suffering," or "patient endurance amidst suffering." Hebrews 11 gives an extensive list of those who patiently suffered hardship. Christ declared, "Blessed are you when men revile you, and persecute you, and say all kinds of evil against you falsely, on account of Me. Rejoice, and be glad, for your reward in heaven is great, for so they persecuted the prophets who were before you" (Matt. 5:11-12; cf. 2 Chron. 36:16; Matt. 23:29-31; Acts 7:52; 1 Thess. 2:15). Jesus Himself has provided the believer with a supreme example of suffering (1 Pet. 2:21-24).

In spite of opposition, the true prophets "spoke in the name of the Lord" (cf. Jer. 44:16); but being spokesmen for God did not exempt them from maltreatment. Mitton observes, "Faithfulness to God's commands so far from giving them immunity from suffering actually involved them in it."[3] If the most eminent of God's people suffered hardship, those of lesser significance should not expect to escape it.

Before introducing the specific example of Job, James states the commonly held and proper estimate of those who were steadfast under adverse circumstances: "We count those blessed [happy] who endured" (v. 11). The present tense suggests that it was common practice to admire those who displayed endurance. Jesus declared, "Blessed are those who have been persecuted for the sake of righteousness" (Matt. 5:10). The articular participle, "those . . . who endured," refers to a general class of sufferers who have shown

3. C. Leslie Mitton, *The Epistle of James* (Grand Rapids: Eerdmans, 1966), 189.

themselves to be steadfast. The verb, whose noun form is used also in 1:3-4, refers to steadfastness under stress (cf. 1:12).

Job is used as an example of such endurance. He is not shown as a man of unrelenting "patience" (*makrothumia*), for he was not always patient with his comforters (Job 3:3; 16:2-4) or with God (Job 10:18; 23:2); but he did have a steadfastness about him in that he remained true to God in spite of his afflictions (Job 1:21-22; 2:10). One must not look only at the endurance of Job but also to the "outcome of the Lord's dealings." "Outcome" (*telos*) can refer either to the conclusion or result of what the Lord did for him, or to the purpose of the Lord's actions. The purpose of the Lord's dealings was to mature Job and bring him to a renewed vision of God's infinite greatness and majesty (Job 42:5-6). The result of His dealings was the blessing of peace and plenty that came to Job after his suffering (Job 42:12-17). Perhaps both ideas are included in the term.

A deeper outcome of endurance in the face of difficulties is a renewed awareness of the character of God. He "is full of compassion and is merciful." We may not always understand the difficult circumstances, but we can rely on the truth of God's infinite mercy. To describe God's tenderness James loosely quotes Psalm 103:8, "The Lord is compassionate and gracious, slow to anger and abounding in lovingkindness" (cf. Ex. 34:6; Pss. 86:15; 145:8). The first adjective, "full of compassion," a compound word meaning "very compassionate," occurs only here in the New Testament. The second adjective, "merciful," though common in the Septuagint, occurs elsewhere only once in the New Testament: "Be merciful, just as your Father is merciful" (Luke 6:36). Awareness of God's compassion will fortify suffering saints in times of need and will help them endure. The rich may not be compassionate, but our God is full of tender mercy.

11

CONCLUDING COUNSEL

James 5:12-20

The use and abuse of the tongue continues to be a primary subject on the author's mind. Believers are not to complain against one another (v. 9) but rather patiently to endure (vv. 10-11). Previously James pictured the tongue as a restless evil full of deadly poison (3:8), which can be used to speak against others (4:11). The mark of a perfect and truly religious person is a bridled tongue (1:26; 3:2). Now in his closing counsel James challenges his readers toward a correct use of the tongue in religious expressions of strong feeling, such as oaths, prayer, praise, confession, and restoration. This last section can be divided into three parts of unequal length: the misuse of oaths (v. 12), the use of prayer and praise (vv. 13-18), and the restoration of a straying member (vv. 19-20).

THE MISUSE OF OATHS (5:12)

Verse 12 forms a fitting transition from what has gone before. The believers have been counseled about proper behavior in the face of overwhelming adversities. The command to refrain from oath-taking forms a natural corollary with the commands to be patient (vv. 7-8) and uncomplaining (v. 9). Rather than swearing (v. 12), the Christian is encouraged to pray when suffering and to praise when cheerful (v. 13).

"Above all" has immediate reference to the sins related to speech, a continuing problem James has addressed. One of the most reprehensible sins of the tongue is to misuse the

Lord's name in an oath. Swearing can take several forms. Impatience can result in using God's name irreverently. That is called profanity. Or one may seek to conceal truth by self-righteously calling upon God to confirm a half-truth. That is blasphemy. Even an honest man can in his own mind be absolutely certain of the veracity of what he is affirming and appeal to God to establish the truth. But that may be bordering on the sin of presumption.

The believer is not to swear "either by heaven or by earth or with any other oath." No doubt James is echoing the words of Jesus (Matt. 5:33-37). The Jews had various subtle ways to distinguish between oaths that were binding and those that were not; thus some would actually use the oath to cheat (Matt. 23:16-22). It is the misuse of oaths that James, following Jesus, condemns. James does not have in mind the rare, solemn, and proper use of the oath, but rather the needless, flippant, and vain use of swearing. Throughout Scripture one can observe the legitimate use of swearing (Gen. 22:16; 1 Kings 17:1; 2 Kings 3:14; Phil. 1:8; Heb. 6:16; Rev. 10:6); but lying, half-truths, and profanity are strictly forbidden.

The basic issue at hand is total honesty in everyday conversation. The member of the Christian community should not need to use an oath to prove the veracity of what he is saying. That would "make some speech more honest than other speech."[1] The injunction should not be understood as a prohibition against official oaths, such as in courts of law or other legal dealings. James, loosely quoting Jesus, continues with the positive manner of expressing truth, "Let your yes be yes, and your no, no" (cf. Matt. 5:37). The apocryphal book of Ecclesiasticus reads:

> Do not inure your mouth to oaths
> or make a habit of naming the Holy One.
> As a slave constantly under the lash
> is never free from weals,

---

1. Davids, 190.

so the man who has oaths and the sacred name
on his lips
will never be clear of guilt.

(23:9-10, NEB)

The reason for making a simple affirmation of yes or no is "so that you may not fall under judgment." That is similar to what was said earlier: "That you yourselves may not be judged," (v. 9). As one should not sigh and complain against another Christian, so one should never swear flippantly or use profanity, for God will judge. In the day of judgment, account will be given for every idle word spoken (Matt. 12:36). Jesus declared that anything beyond a simple yes or no was "of evil" (or "of the evil one," Matt. 5:37).

THE USE OF PRAYER AND PRAISE (5:13-18)

The individual in trying circumstances may be tempted to complain against other believers or to break out in an impious oath, but the proper behavior is to turn to God in prayer. That is the uniting theme of the next six verses. In trouble, joy, or sickness, the response should be prayer. The author speaks first of prayer and praise in times of suffering and good cheer (v. 13), then of prayer in times of specific need (vv. 14-16), and finally gives an illustration of prayer's effectiveness (vv. 17-18).

The subject is introduced by the use of two rhetorical questions, both with a parallel response (v. 13). The effect is like that of the protasis and apodasis of a conditional sentence: "If anyone is suffering, let him pray." Though they may be punctuated as statements of fact, "Someone is suffering; let him pray," the interrogative form seems more in keeping with the context and James's use of questions (2:5-7, 14-16, etc.). "Suffering," the verb form of the noun used of the suffering endured by the prophets (v. 10), refers to calamity or hardship of every sort, whether physical or mental. Paul used it to describe the hardships he had suffered and those that also might befall Timothy (2 Tim. 2:9; 4:5).

Though complaining and grumbling, or even profanity, are

common responses to difficulty, the Christian is to "pray." Scripture promises, "The eyes of the Lord are upon the righteous, and His ears attend to their prayer" (1 Pet. 3:12; cf. Ps. 34:15). The situation itself may not change in response to prayer, but the compassionate God can give the grace necessary to endure (4:6; 2 Cor. 12:9). The one who provides good things (1:17) will supply the wisdom needed to react properly to trials (1:5).

The next rhetorical question speaks of one who is "cheerful," a word used elsewhere in the New Testament only in Acts 27:22, 25. In spite of adverse circumstances, Paul told the sea-tossed seamen, "Keep up your courage." The term does not denote boisterous hilarity, nor does it imply freedom from any form of trouble; it suggests an inner attitude of cheerfulness. In spite of difficult times, the believer can take cheerful courage. Those with such an attitude can respond with songs of praise. The verb "sing praises," originally meant to play the harp, then to sing to the music of a harp, and finally to sing praises with or without instruments. Though used often of singing praises in public worship (1 Cor. 14:15; Eph. 5:19), here the term is probably being used of a more personal and private singing of praise. Whatever the outward circumstances of life, whether good or bad, the Christian can both pray and praise. Paul and Silas, while in the Philippian jail, prayed and sang hymns of praise to God (Acts 16:25).

From the more general "suffering," James now turns to a specific type of suffering for which prayer should be offered (v. 14). "Sick" denotes any illness that debilitates a person for work. It is used primarily of bodily ailments (Matt. 10:8; John 4:46), but it can also refer to mental, emotional, or spiritual sickness or weakness (Rom. 14:1). It has been generally accepted that James uses the term for physical illness, though nonphysical illnesses often have a cause and effect relationship with physical sickness.

The infirm member is not to suffer alone; the aid of church leaders or "elders" is to be sought. The office of elder had its roots both in the structure of the Greek political system and in the organizational structure of the Jewish synagogue. The readers were familiar with the synagogue usage. Though the term may be used for men of advanced age in general, in the church it designates the office of spiritual leadership (Acts 11:30; 20:17; Titus 1:5). Both Peter and John identified themselves as elders (1 Pet. 5:1; 2 John 1).

The elders are "of the church." The term *church* was common both among Jews and Greeks at that time. It was used among the Greeks for a public gathering, whether lawful or unlawful (Acts 19:39, 41), and it occurs commonly in the Septuagint for the assembly of Israel (Deut. 4:10, cf. Acts 7:38). In the New Testament the term is used primarily of the Body of Christ: sometimes of a local church (Phil. 4:15) and elsewhere of the church universal (Eph. 3:10). Here the reference is to a local body (cf. "assembly," *sunagōgēn,* 2:2).

The responsibility of initiating the summons is placed on the sick person: "Let him call." No doubt in the case of serious illness, the family would call the elders. The procedure outlined is evidently to be done at home, not at a church meeting. The main verb, "let them pray," is the central feature, and the participle, "anointing," is subordinate to the main verb. To pray "over him" pictures the elders standing by the sick person and stretching their hands out over him, perhaps extending them upward toward God, in intercessory prayer. The tense of the participle "anointing" does not indicate whether that was done prior to or during the praying. It seems more natural that it would come first, then the prayer.

Anointing "with oil" was often done for medicinal purposes (Isa. 1:6; Luke 10:34), as well as for sacred purposes (Ex. 40:15; Ps. 133:2). Mark 6:13 mentions the twelve "anointing with oil many sick people and healing them." Several interpretations have been given to the practice of anointing. Some see oil as a healing agent, a medical remedy. If that is the sense, James is encouraging the sick to make use of both spiritual and physical means of healing: prayer and oil. However, to anoint "in the name of the Lord" suggests that the anointing was not for medicinal purposes. And further, oil should not be considered the medication for every malady. Another interpretation suggests that it was miraculous healing that occurred during the apostolic age as a supernatural sign to validate the gospel (cf. Mark 6:13). If that were the meaning, though, one would expect the apostles or prophets, not the elders, to be summoned.

Some have suggested that perhaps James mentions oil in the ceremonial healing procedure "in order to reduce the temptation to use charms, incantations, and other such pagan devices."[2] That gives it a Jewish rather than pagan orientation, the Jews being scrupulous in their use of oil. It appears, however, there is more to the anointing than this view gives it.

Still others have proposed that it is "a sacramental vehicle of divine power."[3] But surely there is no spiritual power in the oil itself any more than in the clay Christ made to heal the blind man (John 9:6). The Roman Catholic church has seen in the procedure the sacrament of Extreme Unction, which gives health and strength to the soul, and sometimes to the body, when the individual is in danger of death. But again, one should not see power in the element itself, but in God. Further, James does not indicate that the sick person is near death.

Another view is that oil represents the presence of God, who can accomplish the healing. Finally, oil may be interpreted as an aid to faith, an action of obedience to awaken faith, similar to the Lord's using saliva in His healing ministry (Mark 7:33; 8:23), and Naaman's dipping in the Jordan (2 Kings 5:14). Perhaps it is best understood as symbolic of the healing presence of the Lord used to quicken and awaken faith, both the faith of the elders as well as of the sick person. It is an act of obedience. If, as some suggest, those who are "sick" are not physically ill, but rather spiritually discouraged because of their struggles, then the anointing would be a

---

2. Adamson, 197.
3. Davids, 193.

means whereby the spiritual leaders of the church would bring encouragement to the discouraged saint. Whatever the oil may signify or accomplish, it is clearly not the anointing that does the healing. God does the healing.

The anointing is to be done "in the name of the Lord." That implies a religious act, not solely the application of a medical balm. The phrase "in the name of the Lord," occurring in various forms in the New Testament (Luke 10:17; Acts 3:6; 16:18; 1 Cor. 5:4; Col. 3:17), implies doing the act according to the will and by the authority of Jesus Christ. It further implies that if the person is healed, the cure came from the Lord and not from man (Acts 3:12, 16).

The results of the prayer are healing and forgiveness (v. 15). "The prayer offered in faith" (lit., "the prayer the one offered in faith") points back to the specific prayer offered by the elders. It is to be a prayer of faith—a faith-motivated prayer. The sick one is to exercise faith by calling the elders, the elders by responding to the call, and both can exercise faith as the elders pray. The first result of faith-motivated prayer is restoration. "Restore" (often translated "save") is here usually understood to mean physical healing (cf. Mark 10:52). If the person is not physically sick, but emotionally or spiritually sick, then the restoration is to emotional or spiritual health. Perhaps both are involved, for physical and nonphysical illnesses are often so interrelated that the one will affect the other. The term "sick" (*kamnonta*), a different term than the one used in verse 14 (*asthenei*), refers to weariness, exhaustion, fatigue. The word used earlier (v. 14) refers more to weakness produced by sickness; this word (v. 15) speaks more of the accompanying fatigue. Perhaps it refers to the mental exhaustion and weariness accompanying sickness. Again, if James is addressing the emotionally and spiritually weak, not so much the physically sick, then it denotes the spiritual fatigue that comes because of the oppressions of the rich and other similar pressures.

The faith James mentions must be understood as a reverent, Spirit-motivated trust in a loving Father who does all things well. The prayer must not be a command to or a demand from God; He is our sovereign, we His servants. The Christian takes the position of child to parent. Nor should it be a prayer built on the presumption that one is healed in the atonement, and therefore healing can be claimed and confessed. Granted, prayer should be effective, believing prayer, but God knows best the needs of His own, and physical healing may not be in the child of God's best interest.

Neither the oil nor the prayer should be considered a magical formula for healing. The Lord is the true source: "The Lord will raise him up." The verb "raise up," commonly used for the resurrection (2 Cor. 4:14), refers to the sick person's being enabled to rise to his feet. Using the same verb, Jesus told the paralytic, "Rise, take up your bed, and go home" (Matt. 9:6). If the illness is some form of discouragement, the raising up would be some kind of spiritual uplift given by the Lord to restore and heal the spirit.

We must be careful not to see the formula as a guarantee for physical healing. First, there are certain laws that govern prayer. Prayer must be done in Jesus' name (John 14:13), in faith (Matt. 21:22), according to God's will (1 John 5:14), and with sincerity and earnestness (Matt. 7:7-11). Sin in the heart is a hindrance to prayer (Ps. 66:18), as is disunity (1 Pet. 3:7; cf. Matt. 18:20) and asking with wrong motives (4:3). Second, God does use human instruments and means for healing. Luke was a physician (Col. 4:14), and Paul prescribed a means by which Timothy could find relief from stomach difficulties (1 Tim. 5:23). Third, several in apostolic times were not miraculously healed. Paul sought healing, but God was not pleased to grant it (2 Cor. 12:7-10). Trophimus was not healed (2 Tim. 4:20). When our Lord was at the pool of Bethesda, He chose to heal only one, though there was a multitude of sick and diseased people awaiting healing (John 5:2-9). And fourth, God often allows sickness that through it He might be glorified. That was the case with the blind man (John 9:3) and with the apostle Paul (2 Cor. 12:9-10). Often more praise comes to God through the joyous acceptance of

God's will in suffering than would come if physical healing did occur. Stevenson summarizes:

> In relation to the sick, then, faith does not demand healing in stentorian tones, regardless of inquiry concerning the will of God: faith bows in reverence in His presence, seeking His mind and purpose. If it is His will to heal the sick, He will lead His Spirit-taught servants to utter the prayer of faith for that healing; if that is not His will, then the prayer of faith will be equally Spirit-inspired in its responsive, "Thy will be done."[4]

The additional conditional clause, "If he has committed sins," recognizes that the illness may be from personal sin and points to an additional result of believing prayer. Not all sickness is a result of personal sin (John 9:3), but Scripture is clear that some sickness is (Luke 5:18-25; John 5:14; 1 Cor. 11:30). The perfect, "has committed," pictures one who has committed a sin in the past and is presently living under its consequences. Such a person is given hope and assurance that his sins "will be forgiven him." If a sick person is miraculously healed by God in response to believing prayer, he can be assured that if his illness was caused by sin, those sins have been forgiven. A major portion of the gospel message is the forgiveness of sin, both for the penitent coming to Christ and for the believer who has strayed. David speaks of the healing that came to him when he made confession and received forgiveness (Ps. 32:1-5).

The mention of sins in verse 15 and the general subject of prayer in the context leads to the more general mention of prayer for and confession to one another (v. 16). "Confess" and "pray" are both present tense imperatives denoting that those actions should be general practice. Each verb has the reciprocal pronoun "one another" following it, suggesting an equality, not a hierarchy. The church is a family of equals struggling together against sin and Satan (1 Pet. 5:9), and

---

4. Herbert F. Stevenson, *James Speaks for Today* (Westwood, N.J.: Revell, 1966), 105.

therefore they need to confess to one another and pray for one another. Christians must be wise and use discretion as to the extent of confession. Sins *are* to be confessed, but not so as to cause injury to others; nor should confession be unhealthy exhibitionism. Perhaps the emphasis should be on apologizing and admitting weaknesses one to another so as to heal relationships and bring encouragement to each other. A trusted and understanding friend can be a source of strength and hope. Confession to God, not man, brings forgiveness (1 John 1:9), but confession to a friend can be a source of healing.

The true purpose behind confession and intercession is "that you may be healed." The restoration of verses 14-15 refers specifically to the one who is sick; here the reference is to the more general "you" (plural). The verb *heal* is used both of the healing of the spirit (John 12:40; 1 Pet. 2:24) and the body (Matt. 15:28). Because both physical and spiritual healing are in the context, James may have had both types in mind.

After the call for mutual confession and prayer, there is an affirmation about prayer: "The effective prayer of a righteous man can accomplish much." "Prayer," as translated here, is not the same as the more general term for prayer used four times in the earlier verses (vv. 13, 14, 15, 16*a*). The present word indicates supplication or petition. It is a petition for something personally desired. The petition must come from a "righteous" person to be effective. "Righteous" may be used of one who is right with God in the sense of being justified (Rom. 3:24, 28; 10:10), or of one who acts righteously (James 5:6). John wrote, "The one who practices righteousness is righteous" (1 John 3:7). Here James again calls attention to righteous life-style. The justified man who lives righteously has the potential of an effective prayer life. "Effective" (lit., "in its working") may be taken in an adjectival sense and translated "fervent" or "effective." Or it may be taken either as passive, "when it is made effective, put into operation," or as a middle, "when it is energized, made operational." In any case the meaning is not substantially different. The persevering prayer of a righteous person is effective in that it "can accomplish much" (lit., "is able to do much"). Christ often taught the importance of persistent prayer (Luke 11:5-13; 18:1-8; cf. Matt. 15:22-28).

The teaching on prayer is followed with the example of Elijah (vv. 17-18), a righteous man who did by faith "accomplish much." Elijah, one of the greatest of the prophets, was to be the forerunner of Messiah (Mal. 4:5; cf. Matt. 17:10-11; John 1:21). So important was Elijah in the minds of the Jews that when Jesus cried from the cross, "Eli, Eli," some thought that He was calling for Elijah (Matt. 27:46-47). Though many thought of Elijah as no ordinary person, James reminds his readers that he was first of all a man who had a "nature like ours." "Nature" (*homoiopathēs*) denotes that Elijah was subject to the same human emotion and liable to the same weaknesses that we all have. The word was used by Barnabas and Paul when the mob at Lystra assumed them to be gods: "We are also men of the same nature as you" (Acts 14:15). Though the great Elijah at times allowed his feelings to sway him and depression overwhelm him (1 King 19:4, 10, 14), God answered his prayers.

Two instances of Elijah's praying are given: the prayer for drought (v. 17) and the subsequent prayer for rain (v. 18). "He prayed earnestly" (lit., "with prayer he prayed"), probably means he prayed earnestly and intensely; but it may mean that pray is exactly what he did—he resorted to prayer. The former reflects a Hebrew idiom of intensity like "I have earnestly desired" (Luke 22:15, lit., "with desire I have desired"; cf. John 3:29; Acts 5:28). Though 1 Kings 17:1 does not specifically mention the prayer, the clear declaration "There shall be neither dew nor rain these years, except by my word" implies that Elijah prayed and that God had assured him of the answer. The drought lasted "three years and six months." Though the Old Testament account does not state precisely the duration (cf. 1 Kings 18:1), it appears that its length was a well-known fact of history (Luke 4:25).

"He prayed again" (v. 18) is a summary of what happened on Mount Carmel when Elijah "crouched down on the earth, and put his face between his knees" (1 Kings 18:42). God had promised to send rain (1 Kings 18:1), and the prayer was based on that promise. "The sky [lit., "heaven"] poured rain" can be understood as the sky, the atmospheric heavens, giving rain (cf. Gen. 7:11); or James may be using "heaven" as a reverential synonym for God. Clearly rain is ultimately from God. The benefit of the rain was that "the earth produced its fruit." Rain and crops are often associated with the providential working of God: "He did good and gave you rains from heaven and fruitful seasons, satisfying your hearts with food and gladness" (Acts 14:17).

The illustration of Elijah demonstrates the power of prayer in the life of one who, though beset with human weaknesses, knew the power of prayer. The God who controls nature can restore health to the body and soul of a hurting and discouraged believer.

THE RESTORATION OF A STRAYING MEMBER (5:19-20)

James brings his epistle to an end in an encouraging, supportive, and pastoral manner. In the body there is always the possibility of someone's straying. Such a person needs restoration. Various problems within the body have been introduced, such as the unbridled tongue, unproductive faith, worldly wisdom, quarrels, and presumptuous attitudes—any of which could lead a person astray. So in a tender, pastoral fashion James urges the reclamation and restoration of any who may have strayed.

For the last time the fraternal term "brethren" is used, indicating again the author's loving concern. The picture portrayed, though expressed in hypothetical terms, is clearly one of the possibility, if not the probability, of some individual's straying. The straying of sheep is a familiar metaphor of people's going astray (Isa. 9:16; Ezek. 34:4-5; Heb. 5:2; 1 Pet. 2:25). "Among you" denotes that the erring person is a member of the body. The term "stray" can be understood as deliberately going astray of one's own will or of being led astray by external forces. Perhaps both have happened: the external forces have exerted their influences, and the individual has chosen to wander away from the truth. "Truth" refers to the whole body of the gospel, both the system of truth as well as the moral obligation to it (1:18; 3:14). The term is used in the same manner by Jesus (John 8:32; 16:13), Paul (Gal. 5:7; 2 Thess. 2:10), and John (1 John 3:19).

James does not issue a command that someone turn the wandering one back, but rather assumes that someone will. The indefinite "one" makes clear that the duty of restoration is not limited to elders or other church officers, but that it is the rightful concern of each member of the body, just as prayer is (v. 16). No mention is made of procedures for reclamation, but loving confrontation, intercessory prayer, forgiveness, and positive acceptance would certainly be in order (see 2 Cor. 2:7-11). If the individual who has strayed is a true believer, he needs to be restored to fellowship; if he has only been an apparent believer, he needs to be brought to salvation and then welcomed into the body.

There is a blessing in restoring someone to fellowship (v. 20). "Let him know" is based on an uncertain reading. Some suggest the second person plural, either the imperative "know ye" or the indicative "you know." In keeping with the flow of the passage, the third person imperative "let him know" seems to fit best. The one who is straying is a "sinner"; he has wandered from the truth. "His way" and "the truth" (v. 19) are contrasted. An individual either walks in God's truth or in his own way. The two, truth and error (the noun form of the verb "stray"), are mutually exclusive: either one walks in truth according to the spirit of truth, or he strays and is obedient to the spirit of error (1 John 4:6).

The results of restoration are twofold: "Will save his soul from death, and will cover a multitude of sins." "Soul" refers to the immaterial, inner life of a person; "save" to spiritual salvation and restoration; and "death" to eternal, spiritual death. Those terms express the seriousness of wandering away. Does James then teach the loss of salvation of a true believer? Burdick notes, "Since Scripture teaches that once a person is regenerated he can never be lost, it may be assumed that [t]his hypothetical wanderer is not a genuine believer."[5] He is evidently one who has been related to the Christian community through a superficial profession of faith, similar to those of whom John writes: "They went out from us, but they were not really of us; for if they had been of us, they would have remained with us; but they went out, in order that it might be shown that they all are not of us" (1 John 2:19). If the one who has strayed is a believer, the death spoken of would of necessity be physical death (1 Cor. 5:5; 11:30). In either case believers in the body dare not overlook the seriousness of one of their members' wandering from the truth (Matt. 18:12-14).

The concept of "cover" is a Hebrew idiom meaning "forgive" (Ps. 85:2). David wrote, "How blessed is he whose transgression is forgiven, whose sin is covered" (Ps. 32:1; cf. Rom. 4:7). Whoever the erring one may be, whatever the gravity or number of the sins committed, the blood of Jesus is available as a covering. No one is hopeless, for the atonement is for all (1 John 2:2). Some have thought that the person whose sins are covered is the restorer. In that sense the one who does the pastoral work of restoration is assured that his own sins will be covered because he cared about someone else. However, to achieve any kind of forgiveness for works done is unscriptural. There is clearly a blessedness in seeing one restored, but the sins covered are those of the one restored.

James started his epistle by encouraging those being sorely tried to be joyful; he concludes with the blessedness of restoration and forgiveness. His pastoral heart longs for the reclamation of any struggling believer who has wandered away from the truth.

The Great Shepherd revealed His pastoral heart when He

---

5. Donald W. Burdick, *James, The Expositor's Bible Commentary,* ed. Frank E. Gabelein (Grand Rapids: Zondervan, 1981), 12:205.

said to Peter, "Simon, Simon, behold, Satan has demanded permission to sift you like wheat; but I have prayed for you, that your faith may not fail; and you, when once you have turned again, strengthen your brothers" (Luke 22:31-32). Some days later, after the resurrection, Peter was restored; and Jesus, in response to Peter's love, commissioned him with a pastoral ministry: "Tend My sheep" (John 21:17). What a challenge for the church today!

BIBLIOGRAPHY

Adamson, James B. *The Epistle of James. The New International Commentary on the New Testament.* Edited by F. F. Bruce. Grand Rapids: Eerdmans, 1981.

Burdick, Donald W. *James.* Vol. 12 of *The Expositor's Bible Commentary.* Edited by Frank E. Gaebelein. Grand Rapids: Zondervan, 1981.

Davids, Peter H. *The Epistle of James. The New International Greek Testament Commentary.* Edited by I. Howard Marshall and W. Ward Gasque. Grand Rapids: Eerdmans, 1982.

Dibelius, Martin. *A Commentary on the Epistle of James. Hermeneia: A Critical and Historical Commentary on the Bible.* Edited by Helmut Koester. Revised by Heinrich Greeven. Translated by Michael A. Williams. Philadelphia: Fortress, 1976.

Eusebius, Pamphilus. *The Ecclesiastical History of Eusebius Pamphilus.* Translated by Christian Frederick Cruse. Grand Rapids: Baker, 1962.

Hiebert, D. Edmond. *The Epistle of James: Tests of a Living Faith.* Chicago: Moody, 1979.

Johnstone, Robert. *Lectures Exegetical and Practical on the Epistle of James.* Grand Rapids: Baker, 1954.

Josephus, Flavius. "The Antiquities of the Jews." In *The Works of Falvius Josephus.* Translated by William Whiston. Edinburgh: William P. Nimmo, n.d.

Lange, John Peter, and Van Oosterzee, J. J. *The Epistle General of James. Lange's Commentary on the Holy Scriptures.* Edited by John Peter Lange. Translated by J. Isador Mombert. Grand Rapids: Zondervan, n.d.

Laws, Sophia. *A Commentary on the Epistle of James. Harper's New Testament Commentaries.* New York: Harper and Row, 1980.

Lenski, R. C. H. *The Interpretation of the Epistle to the Hebrews and the Epistle of James*. Minneapolis: Augsburg, 1966.

Mayor, Joseph B. *The Epistle of St. James. Classic Commentary Library*. Grand Rapids: Zondervan, 1954.

Mitton, C. Leslie. *The Epistle of James*. Grand Rapids: Eerdmans, 1966.

Oesterley, W. E. *The General Epistle of James*. Vol. 4 of *The Expositor's Greek Testament,* edited by W. Robertson Nicoll. Grand Rapids: Eerdmans, 1951.

Ropes, James Hardy. *A Critical and Exegetical Commentary on the Epistle of St. James. The International Commentary on the Holy Scriptures of the Old and New Testaments.* Edited by Alfred Plummer and Francis Brown. Edinburgh: T. & T. Clark, 1978.

Ross, Alexander. *The Epistles of James and John. The New International Commentary on the New Testament*. Edited by F. F. Bruce. Grand Rapids: Eerdmans, 1972.

Stevenson, Herbert F. *James Speaks for Today*. Westwood, N.J.: Revell, 1966.

Tasker, R. V. G. *The General Epistle of James*. Vol. 16 of *The Tyndale New Testament Commentaries*. Edited by R. V. G. Tasker. Grand Rapids: Eerdmans, 1980.

Wessel, Walter W. "The Epistle of James." In *The Wycliffe Bible Commentary*. Edited by Charles F. Pheiffer and Everett F. Harrison. Chicago: Moody, 1976.

Moody Press, a ministry of the Moody Bible Institute, is designed for education, evangelization, and edification. If we may assist you in knowing more about Christ and the Christian life, please write us without obligation: Moody Press, c/o MLM, Chicago, Illinois 60610.